HEART TREE FOR EMPTY NESTERS

BY SHERRY KUGHN

Lambert Book House
4139 Parkway Drive
Florence, Alabama 35630

All scripture quotations, unless otherwise indicated, are taken from the
King James Version of the Holy Bible.

Published by
Lambert Book House
4139 Parkway Drive
Florence, Alabama 35630

ISBN 978-0-89315-421-9

Printed in the United States of America

CONTENTS

Prologue 6

Faith

CHAPTER 1 11

CHAPTER 2 21

CHAPTER 3 33

CHAPTER 4 45

Hope

CHAPTER 5 57

CHAPTER 6 69

CHAPTER 7 81

CHAPTER 8 91

Love

CHAPTER 9 103

CHAPTER 10 113

CHAPTER 11 125

CHAPTER 12 135

Faith, Hope, Love

CHAPTER 13 145

Dedication

This book is dedicated to my mother,

Sarah Parker Ford,

and my mother-in-law,

Louise Reitzell Kughn.

Prologue

The afternoon was lovely – twenty-five Christian women of all ages sitting in a circle near a swimming pool brightened with nearby strands of hot-pink, bougainvillea flowers. The speaker finished her devotional talk and asked for prayer requests. A finger went up. "Remember my son and his family who stopped attending church." The wave of a hand caught the speaker's eye. "My daughter is having marriage troubles." Another voice spoke as a throat cleared. "Pray that my son will become a Christian."

Such requests have been common in every devotional for women I have ever attended – mother after mother asks for prayers for her adult children. I hear the requests also in Sunday school classes, at women's retreats, over lunch. No matter what ages are the mothers or their children, the mothers' hearts are always concerned about their children.

I think often, too, about my own requests to God. I have three adult children now. I do not feel very influential in their lives anymore, especially their spiritual lives; yet I continue to pray for them to be Christ-like. I pray about a new dimension in my family – my young in-laws. I love them in the same ways as I love my own children, but I feel even less influential in their lives.

I realize that to influence anyone in a positive way for Christ, especially my children, I must be a happy, fulfilled, well-balanced Christian. I must also be like Christ – humble and wise. With my children, I must be honest and willing to face and confront my past and current mistakes. I do not excel at any of those things, but as in all levels of Christian living, I am most effective when I am striving to be like Christ.

I spend less and less time with my children as life moves along. I visit them: they visit me, now with their families in tow. During both visits, I have little one-on-one time with each adult child. They leave, and I long for a time when I know we can lavishly share time together again, even more than we did when they were small. That time probably won't come until we are in heaven.

When the children were growing up, they often teased me about a motto I made up because I repeated it so often. The motto fit, though, because it made us focus on the most important things we did each day rather than on the avalanche of details involved in their busy, young lives. "Stay faithful to God, be happy, be loving:" that was my motto. I tried then and still do try to fulfill the motto myself. Occasionally, I still remind my adult children from time to time of the motto's soundness, especially when I see them struggling with the same "avalanche of details" that I dealt with back then – back during the 1970s-80s when I raised children. The motto is timeless, though. It could apply to any age, even an age as challenging as the 2000s.

I think back to the women's devotional by the pool. We all seemed that day to be seeking the same answers to the question of how we could encourage and influence our adult children to live the Christian life. Some members of our group weren't Christians during the times they raised children. What can they do about that now? All of us made mistakes in raising children, even the most faithful among us. Those among us who raised our children "in the church" would never brag that we did the job right. We have all learned that the job of mothering is not a thing that can be done perfectly, as someone baking a perfect cake. We know that sometimes even the perfect cake can fall apart as we stand and admire it.

So, I begin a journey to study ways that we, as mature Christian mothers, can encourage adult children to live the Christian life. I have friends who want answers to their concerns, but mostly, I study and write these things for myself. I want to know how to address the difficult issues of being a Christian mother and grandmother in postmodern times when not many things in life seem connected to truth, to the Bible, or to God or Jesus.

The Bible says three of the most important aspects of life are faith, hope, and love. The following study lessons are divided into these three topics — four lessons on each and then a final chapter of review. I pray that, as a mother, your heart is encouraged when communicating with and loving your adult children, and I pray that you and I both grow in our knowledge of the faith, hope, and love God has for each of us.

Chapter
1

A mother's heart is like a tree.

She wants her adult children,

like birds, to fly in and out

of her life as often as necessary

to keep alive the faith and love that

established the home.

In her book, *Gifts from the Sea*, author Anne Morrow Lindbergh described her feelings about her children leaving home with a metaphor about the Argonaut's shell. "It is a cradle for the young, held in the arms of the mother Argonaut who floats with it to the surface, where the eggs hatch and the young swim away. Then the mother Argonaut leaves her shell and starts another life" (95).

I love the image of a mother who breaks suddenly with the old and starts anew. Who but God, though, knows how a mother Argonaut truly feels? The break with my children was more gradual, for which I was grateful. They, like most modern adult children, went away to college or to a new job, and they often visited back home. They stayed in touch, too, by way of telephones and computers. These modern customs and innovations were good for me because they gave me the opportunity to adopt gradually a new lifestyle.

Another metaphorical comparison we mothers share with trees is that we have grown tall through life's experiences; that is, we have perspective. Many of us are freer and less burdened than during our child-rearing days. In fact, we can sometimes feel as free as leaves appear when blowing in the wind and reflecting the light of the sun. Ideally, mature Christian mothers stand independent, happy, and fulfilled; and friends and family of all ages feel free to fly in and out of the branches of our hearts and enjoy the wisdom we gained from raising our children.

One of my favorite heart-tree experiences happened when my middle child changed jobs. He and his family lived briefly with my husband and me for a month, and I was happy that they seemed to fly in, feel right at home, and nest for a while —a short while, thankfully.

I am glad I can say "thankfully." The words show I have adapted to "life without children." I consider the achievement a milestone. All the characteristics I share with a tree are ones that have not come easily. I emerged from the anguish of the empty-nest syndrome in or near the year 2000. Before then, I wondered if I could ever be happy again without my children living at home. I was not a tree back then: I was a nest with a giant hole in the center.

I remember a particular summer afternoon as I think back on those painful days, which actually started around 1987 when my firstborn child began driving (and I realized he would soon "drive" out of my life). My son had moved to college. He came home for a visit, and I heard a commotion outside the back door. I peeked through the window where his brother and sister, both 18 at the time, were doubled over laughing. I stepped outside and looked down from our back deck onto a tree that had been lopped off by a utility lineman earlier in the day. My son, then about 20, was sitting in the middle of the tree mimicking a giant bird in a nest. He flapped his elbows, squawked loudly, and wiggled his imaginary "tail feathers." We laughed more and more the longer we looked at him. It was not only his imitation of a bird that was funny but also the garish size of this "bird and nest." Finally, unable to laugh anymore, I turned to go back indoors, and to my surprise I began crying.

I hurried to my bedroom so I wouldn't spoil the fun for the children, and I cried alone. I wondered how one of the funniest things I had ever seen made me so sad.

Looking back, I realized I hurt for two reasons: the fun we had had as a family was about to end as all three children were preparing to leave home. My son's imitation of a bird was a gigantic reminder of the imminent "death" of my family. I was in grief, yet I did not want the children to know. I turned to the Bible.

In Matthew 13:31,32, Jesus tells of a mustard plant that grows from a tiny seed. It becomes "a tree, so that the birds of the air come and lodge in the branches thereof."

Most Biblical scholars believe the plant in the scriptures was the *brassica nigra,* which is different from today's prevalent mustard plant. *Brassica nigra,* named after its black seeds, grew in the Palestine area, and the tiny seeds were often sewn in the fields. The *brassica nigra* grew large enough to provide great nesting places for birds and provided seeds for them to eat.

Today, ground mustard seeds can be used for a poultice or used to extract oil. The leaves, which are full of vitamins and minerals, can be cooked and eaten. (Mother Nature is practical like the rest of us mothers.)

Even the most devout Christian parents are not wise enough during the child-raising years to raise children without inflicting and receiving some emotional pain and conflict. Thus, our goal after the children are raised should be to overcome the scars from these conflicts and to change the adult-child relationship into a friendship.

In the Bible, one great example of a woman who became "a heart tree" is Naomi in the book of Ruth, who learned to cultivate a heart open to communication and fellowship with her daughter-in-law. In the opening of the book, the Bible tells the story of Naomi, a mother in grief over her deceased husband and sons. Naomi's faith in God and in His power to improve her circumstances fostered a relationship with her daughter-in-law Ruth. Naomi's heart was honest: she admitted bitterness toward God. Naomi's heart was generous: she offered Ruth a home. Naomi's heart was wise: she respected and observed the laws and customs of her

> *Our goal after the children are raised should be to overcome the scars from these conflicts and to change the adult-child relationship into a friendship.*

land and offered Ruth advice about how to win Boaz's love. Naomi did not stop cultivating her heart after she lost her own sons. She humbly persevered, maintained her faith, overcame difficulties, and embraced her new circumstances. Her daughter-in-law became like a daughter, and Ruth trusted Naomi to care for Obed, the baby who would become the grandfather to King David.

Another example of a mother and a grandmother being "heart trees" is found in the story of Eunice and Lois. In the opening of the second book of Timothy, Paul speaks of the godly reputation of these women. They were Paul's friends and possibly introduced him to Timothy, their son and grandson, who became one of the first ministers in the early church. Because of the godliness these two women taught Timothy, their role in God's plan for the early church was as important as Timothy's role.

A third example of a godly mother refers to a little-known character in the New Testament named Rufus. He and his mother, whose name is not revealed, were praised by the apostle Paul in Romans 16:13. "Salute Rufus chosen in the Lord, and his mother and mine," said Paul. Think what kinds of service this mother performed for Paul and her son, both of whom were involved in a project as important as spreading the gospel – cooking, serving, encouraging, changing beds, praying, giving of her means, missing out on sleep, etc. We mothers know what was involved in her service to these early Christians because we know how busy we become when even one of our offspring takes on big projects.

All of these examples show us that mothers in the Bible stayed involved in their adult children's lives in appropriate ways.

Scripture Readings and Prayers

1. Naomi found great blessings in her daughter-in-law, Ruth.

🕊 **Reading:** Ruth, chapters 1-4 teaches about the joys and anguish experienced by this godly mother.

🕊 **Prayer:** "Dear Heavenly Father, please turn the painful experiences we have as mothers into blessings."

2. Eunice and Lois taught their son and grandson, Timothy, to also serve God.

🕊 **Reading:** 2 Timothy 1 tells us about the positive spirit of appreciation that Paul paid to his fellow Christians.

🕊 **Prayer:** "Dear Heavenly Father, allow Your light to be seen in us by our children and by those outside the family."

3. Paul thanked several women for their devotion to Christ's kingdom.

🕊 **Reading:** Romans 16:1-16 tells us of the importance of women in the early church.

🕊 **Prayer:** "Dear Heavenly Father, help us to not only teach our children about leadership in the church but also to show them how we can be leaders in Your kingdom."

4. These "universal mothers" will always be remembered as "heart trees" because their service to God was recorded in the Bible, a blessing unknown to them at the time. In the same way, our efforts to others in God's kingdom may be felt for the rest of eternity.

🕊 **Reading:** Acts 18:18-26 tells us about Priscilla; Acts 9:36-43 tells us about Dorcas/Tabitha.

🕊 **Prayer:** "Dear Heavenly Father, help us to serve You for the sake of doing what is right and knowing You may use our example to help others."

Mother Oaks
Stand Strong

Dottie Travis, now widowed, provided care for more than 50 years for her son, Rob, who has cerebral palsy. Rob lives at Rainbow Omega home for developmentally delayed adults in Eastaboga, Alabama. Dottie also has a daughter, Glenda, and a son-in-law, Dan, both of whom worked at Rainbow Omega.

"I never resented the fact that Rob was handicapped. He was so precious to my husband Bob and me. We always learned a lot from him. He was cheerful and made us develop a lot of patience. I've always been a homemaker, so being a mother to both of my children was my career. I had Glenda nine months to the day after I married, which suited me just fine."

Even Weeping
Willows Smile

My husband tells the story of a grandson who spoke at his grandmother's funeral. He remembered running into her home with a bloody nose inflicted by a teen-aged boy. His grandmother grabbed her purse, stalked across the nearby baseball field to where the boy was, and began whacking him with her purse. The grandson said he couldn't help but laugh as the boy first tried to defend himself and then turned and ran away. "Grandma really stood up for us kids," he said.

Chapter
2

A mother's heart is like

the heart of a hen:

she will sacrifice everything

for her children.

A farmer strolled across his property to inspect it after a grass fire. As he walked back toward his house, he spotted an ashy, burned stump in the field. He stepped back and kicked the stump with his foot. A dozen baby chicks ran in many different directions. Stunned, the farmer looked closer. The stump was actually a dead mother hen who had gathered her babies beneath her wings to save them from the fire.

Mothers can identify with the hen. At times, we have all felt as if the rigors of parenting were "burning" us. At times, we have all been tired, anxious, and stressed in order to protect and nurture our children. Thankfully, most of us are not physically "burned" during the process, but no one escapes without a few scars.

Motherhood is sometimes a thankless job, too. Children never understand the sacrifices we have made until they grow up and become parents. Even then, some adult children become unappreciative, destructive adults; and even if the mother is not at fault concerning her children's difficult issues, she blames herself. The resulting guilt can drag her life down to an equal or worse level of destruction than what her children experience. God does not want a mother to live that way.

Below are three true stories (with names changed) from friends who learned how a mother's heart is tied to her children's lives:

"I don't want to live anymore," said Deidre, a friend I knew for years from the time when our children were in first grade together. "My daughters never call, they steal drugs from my medicine cabinet, and they are in and out of jail. It is embarrassing to have girls who have turned out like this, and why? I gave them everything I could when they were little, and is this the thanks I get?"

"I was a terrible mother," Annette said. "I don't know what I was thinking when I left my sons alone so much. I found out years later that bad things went on in our neighborhood while I was at work and then, after work, at parties. My older son is in prison sentenced to life without parole, and my second son suffers with the anxiety and depression that follows drug addiction. I can never be happy. I feel guilty if I even try to smile about something."

"My daughter told me she hates me, and she hates the way I raised her," Maxine told me on the phone one day when I called her after she had had a heart attack. "She won't visit me. She won't come near me because she says this Christian life I have lived is too judgmental. I raised her too strictly, and she tells me she will resent me until the day I die."

I remember hurting along with my friends as I listened to each of their problems. I never knew how to advise them. I still don't, but God does. He can help mothers with big problems.

God can help mothers who suffer with depression. Many older mothers suffer from medical conditions related to mood disorders, and many older mothers suffer because of sin — their own or someone else's. Counseling with a medical doctor can resolve physical depression. Counseling with a spiritual mentor or a trained counselor can resolve emotional and spiritual depression. Medication or psychotherapy can help resolve physical depression, too. Forgiving others and forgiving ourselves can resolve spiritual depression. But neglecting these conditions leads to health problems and destroyed lives.

> *Forgiving others and forgiving ourselves can resolve spiritual depression.*

God can help mothers who feel overwhelmed when facing problems that plague today's children. Life is hard. Our society is saturated with many of life's worst problems: drug additions, pollution, and moral decline. Yet, in many ways, we are better off than in past times due to improvements in medicine, economics, communication, transportation, and food production.

How do Christians make sense of these extremes?

The answer is that we should focus on the positive aspects of life. We should not try to solve things outside of our control. Instead, we should acknowledge that God is still in control of His children's lives. Romans 8:25-27 shows us how our hopes and God's Spirit work together to accomplish His will. The scripture says, "But if we hope for that we see not, then do we with patience wait for it. Likewise the Spirit also helpeth our infirmities: for we know not what we should pray for as we ought: but the Spirit itself maketh intercession for us with groanings which cannot be uttered. And he that searcheth the hearts knoweth what is the mind of the Spirit, because he maketh intercession for the saints according to the will of God." If the Spirit intercedes to God for us, then our role is simply to pray and to wait.

Moses, who was a loving parental figure to the children of Israel, once faced a tumultuous sea on one side and an advancing army on the other. He looked to God who gave him a way to escape this dilemma. Joseph was thrown into a dungeon and waited on God to arrange his release. He, too, looked to God and found a way to escape a terrible situation. Job suffered the loss of his family and his possessions. He was forced to sit outdoors in ashes, and he was covered with boils. Job looked to God and waited on Him for help. If the people of the Old Testament can thrive in spite of problems, then Christian mothers can do the same and more — Christian mothers have Jesus.

If Jesus is in a mother's heart, He can erase guilt over past mistakes. Christian mothers can find forgiveness from their adult children by asking for it. Most adult children are eager to forgive their parents because they love them. Adult children struggling to raise their own children certainly will better understand the mistakes their parents made. Christian mothers who struggle with guilt often fail to forgive themselves.

In Luke 1:78,79, Zechariah sang a song of praise to God when he learned that he would be a father: "Through the tender mercy of our God; whereby the dayspring from on high hath visited us, to give light to them that sit in darkness and in the shadow of death, to guide our feet into the way of peace." The New International Version of the Bible uses the word "rising sun" instead of the word "dayspring" for Jesus. Both are lovely images. God's son (and "rising sun") was still in Mary's womb as Zechariah sang these words. Without ever having met Jesus, Zechariah knew what Jesus' role would be.

God can also work on adult children's hearts. He can help even those adult children who reject their parents and Him. Throughout people's lives, God calls them to Him. He uses good and bad situations and people's weaknesses and strengths to bring them by life's end to the realization that He should be the most important person to them. God is not an egotist, but His importance in people's lives determines whether or not they become who He wants them be. God calls His children to Him, no matter their age. Mothers can assist God by coming to Him and by encouraging their adult children to come to Him, even if no words are ever spoken but only actions and faith are displayed.

Thankfully, in the three examples of distraught mothers mentioned early in this chapter, two of the three situations have been resolved with happy (earthly) endings. Deidre sought and received help for her depression. Also, her children matured and began raising children of their own. Deidre is happier than ever

God can also work on adult children's hearts. He can help even those adult children who reject their parents and Him.

and pursues her own dreams and goals, and she enjoys the company of her adult children and her grandchildren.

Maxine's daughter's life spiraled downward into drug addiction. When her daughter sought rehabilitation, Maxine assisted, and the two grew closer than ever.

Annette's health problems worsened, but not before she asked forgiveness from her two sons. Afterward, another heart attack claimed her life. Both sons became Christians, and even though one remains in prison, he works with the prison ministry. I feel confident for all three mothers that even happier endings will be revealed when earth life is over.

Scripture Readings and Prayers

1. The author of Psalm 119 (possibly David) knew much heartache. Verse 143 says, "Trouble and anguish have taken hold on me: yet thy commandments are my delights."

   ❧ **Reading:** David counterbalanced his songs of anxiety, fear, depression, and grief with songs of praise. How do we counterbalance our troubles?

   ❧ **Prayer:** "Dear Heavenly Father, help us to focus on You and Your commands throughout our lives, no matter what heartaches and delights we experience as mothers."

2. In Exodus, after releasing the children of Israel, the Egyptian pharaoh pursued them, his army of warriors driving chariots toward seemingly helpless men, women, and children.

   ❧ **Reading:** Exodus 14. Events surrounding the Israelites crossing the Red Sea.

   ❧ **Prayer:** "Dear Heavenly Father, we as mothers are terrified at times because of the circumstances faced by us and our children. Please help us to 'be still' and trust You, having faith that You will direct our steps."

3. Joseph faced big troubles throughout his life, especially when dealing with his brothers' hatred.

🕊 **Reading:** Genesis 37:3,4 and 17-28. Even through such grave hardships, God helped Joseph have a victorious life.

🕊 **Prayer:** "Dear Heavenly Father, help us rejoice when our troubles are small and help us depend on You when they are many. When troubles enter our families, help us to apply Your laws of love to resolve them."

By actions
and faith, mothers
can assist God
by coming to Him and
by encouraging their
adult children
to come to
Him.

Mother Oaks Stand Strong

Diane Carpenter is a wife and mother who has worked closely alongside her husband Stentson to establish Rainbow Omega, an assisted living facility and home that provides award-winning care and services to dozens of mentally challenged adults. The Carpenters' motivation for establishing Rainbow Omega was their love for son Chris and others like him who will most likely outlive their parents. The Carpenters are also the parents of another son, Mike, who has given them three grandchildren.

"Motherhood is the greatest joy and the gravest responsibility a woman can have. Joy is when you see your children's influence on others and see them helping to change a life. To see the influence Chris has had on people he has touched with only his smile is wonderful. To watch Mike teach his children about God and to see the love he shows each child is pure joy for me."

Even Weeping Willows Smile

Greenbrier Church member Gail Carden said her daughter Julie came home from college after the first semester, opened the back door of their house, and stepped into the most abundant patio garden her mother had ever grown. "What are all these flowers about?" she asked her mother. "Is this a sign of the empty nest?"

Notes

Chapter
3

After her children leave home,

a mother's heart is like an empty nest;

yet, God can fill her heart

when she seeks fulfillment

from her faith in Him.

From childhood I have visited an exhibit of rare birds and their nests in my hometown of Anniston, Alabama. William Werner of Atlantic City, New Jersey, collected and preserved them during the latter part of the 19th century. Businessman Severn Regar bought the collection and moved it to Anniston in 1930, where he created the Regar Museum. Later, the collection became a part of the acclaimed Anniston Museum of Natural History.

From childhood I marveled at the bird nests in the collection, some the size of a dime and others the size of a straw hat. Many of the nests have eggs and baby birds. My fascination with them confirmed my focus on motherhood from early childhood. Before I had children, motherhood was the number one "job" I wanted. Looking back, motherhood was the most rewarding and challenging "job" I have ever had. My children fulfilled my heart when they lived at home and left my heart empty when they were gone. It did not take me long after the children moved away, though, to realize that my empty heart was a drain on their emotions. I could hear over the telephone the anxiety in their voices when I would share with them my struggles related to the empty nest. I could also hear their desire to be independent during their college days. Nothing seemed to please them more than knowing I was moving on, developing my own interests, and doing things I never had time to do when they were living at home.

God, as always, helped me survive that difficult time. Reading the Psalms helped me. My women's Sunday school class and the church became more important to me. Nothing filled the emptiness within my heart like Christian music and the prayer time I developed with God. I didn't know it then, but my heart was healing, developing a special place that knew not only serenity during a time of great pain but also joy. The faith that had always been a part of me since childhood became more important.

In his book, *Secret Place of Joy*, author and musician Lindell Cooley says he once learned that his administrative assistant had endured two divorces without mentioning her difficult circumstances to him. When he asked her how she had managed to be so happy, even joyful at work each day, she told him she had developed a special place within her heart that belonged to the Lord. "He became my husband," she told him. "He became my friend, my healer and my everything." (116) That place is the same one, writes Cooley, that King David wrote about in Psalms 16:11. "In thy presence is fullness of joy; at thy right hand there are pleasures for evermore."

"In thy presence is fullness of joy; at thy right hand there are pleasures for evermore."
— Psalms 16:11

I realized during those recovery years that God was filling that empty place in my heart with His presence. The empty nest syndrome for me lasted a little more than ten years. I, as a little girl who had wanted nothing more than to be a "mommy," was finally a mature Christian woman. I began to seek fulfillment in new ways beyond my duties as a mother. My call had gone full circle. I felt healed, whole, and complete as a human being. And now, rather than being finished with parenthood, it has taken on new and wonderful meaning — an achievement brought about by God.

The mature Christian mother has the opportunity to become a universal parent to others outside of her family. She can help and teach children of all ages because she has gained experience. She can better understand and love other (even undesirable) adults when she tries to visualize them as children and how God has loved them from childhood. Universal parenthood is a role that God understands. His role to humans, as the God of earth, is to rear them. In *Webster's New Twentieth Century Dictionary*, the word "rear" is a verb that means "to bring up or to raise to maturity; to foster; to cherish; to nurse; to educate; to instruct." According to the dictionary, the word "rear" also means "to rise high, as a mountain peak." We mothers understand that first definition, but isn't the latter a beautiful idea that is very closely related to what God wants from us? He wants us to become a mountain peak, as He is, so we can help others as He does.

I visited an aunt throughout my life who, at various times, lived in Seattle, Washington and Portland, Oregon. No matter where I traveled in both cities, I gained comfort, a sense of awe, an appreciation for beauty, and encouragement when I looked up and saw the lovely chain of snow-capped mountains.

In the same way, our own children will view us favorably if and when they see us becoming universal parents growing in God's character and love. This happens when they see us helping other people, praying with young people, and encouraging parents of children outside the family unit. We help our own adult children when we allow them the time, space, and freedom from guilt as they leave our homes. The only way our adult children can truly begin to grow is when they cut themselves free from us. Sometimes, the only way they can be free is when we remove our focus from their lives and refocus by helping others and improving our own character.

The only way our adult children can truly begin to grow is when they cut themselves free from us.

One of the best discoveries many Christian mothers make after their children leave home is self-discovery.

For the first time ever in many women's lives, they have time to pursue personal interests. They have time to exercise their bodies, develop their minds, spend time with husbands, tend to family members, pursue a dream job, and travel to special places — the pursuits are wide open and different for each woman.

I found an unexpected delight in overcoming the empty nest when I discovered who my children became as adults. After they left home for college, each of them also married, had children, and worked at jobs. Now it is wonderful to observe them as spouses, parents, and employees. The time we now spend together is rare but appreciated by each of us. When they were living at home, I had to be a disciplinarian. I had to push them away to encourage independence and pull them close to let them know I cared. They pushed me away to grow, and they sometimes pulled me near them when they struggled with life. This pushing and pulling within our relationships eventually ended. Now our time together feels like a giant hug.

The best delight of all, though, is becoming a grandparent. We already know how brief childhood is and how we can treasure and encourage the spirit of a child. No one knows more than a grandparent the joy of staring into the eyes of someone who thinks you were created just to play with them — to run barefoot through the grass, to sniff new crayons together, or to squish clay with our fingers. Young parents must focus on providing for their children and becoming mature adults, and since (most) grandparents are already mature, they have the luxury of focusing only on the spirit inside each of the grandchildren.

It is amazing to me, too, that one of the best ways to encourage our adult children is to show them that life after their children are raised can be more fulfilling than ever.

One of the best ways to encourage our adult children is to show them that life after their children are raised can be more fulfilling than ever.

The attitude a Christian mother should have after her offspring leaves home should be the same as the Bible character Hannah in 1 Samuel 1-2. In the Bible story, Hannah wanted a child but had been unable to conceive. While on an annual trip with her husband Elkanah, she prayed about her grief in God's temple. Hannah's sorrowful countenance and heartbreaking utterances so struck the priest Eli that he first accused her of being drunk. He then listened as she explained the reason for her grief. She promised Eli in God's presence that she would give her firstborn son for service in God's temple. Eli said her request for a child would be granted. Hannah's joy in having her son Samuel was great. Nowhere, though, do we read that she regretted having made the commitment of returning him to God. Never do we read that she grieved leaving him at the temple or that she ever attempted to bring him back home. In fact, the only other stories in the Bible about Hannah are that she brought to her son a new robe each year and that she conceived five more children. Hannah filled the void left by Samuel's leaving by raising more children. She didn't abandon Samuel; she maintained an annual connection with her son. If only we Christian mothers had the faith of Hannah – the faith to dedicate our children to God even before they are born, the faith to follow through on our promises to be faithful to God in all circumstances, and the ability to keep appropriate connections to our children after they are gone – would not the church flourish in ways we've only dreamed?

Scripture Readings and Prayers

1. King David was "a man after God's own heart." He knew the joy that only God can give.

❧ **Reading:** Psalms 126:5,6. "They that sow in tears shall reap in joy. He that goeth forth and weepeth, bearing precious seed, shall doubtless come again with rejoicing, bringing his sheaves with him."

❧ **Prayer:** "Dear Heavenly Father, please reward the efforts we sometimes painfully sow when raising children so that we can enjoy the fruits of our labors."

2. The author of Hebrews defined what faith is. Mothers can apply the definition to their efforts of raising their children.

🕊 **Reading**: Hebrews 11:1. "Now faith is the substance of things hoped for, the evidence of things not seen."

🕊 **Prayer**: "Dear Heavenly Father, help us have faith in the wonderful things we desire for our children and have faith in our relationships with them. Help us to understand the things not seen are the most valuable."

3. Hannah's faith in her son's future is an inspiration to mothers.

🕊 **Reading**: 1 Samuel 1:11. "And she vowed a vow, and said, O Lord of hosts, if thou wilt indeed look on the affliction of thine handmaid, and remember me, and not forget thine handmaid, but wilt give unto thine handmaid a man child, then I will give him unto the Lord all the days of his life."

🕊 **Prayer**: "Dear Heavenly Father, help us to do what we can at any age to encourage our children to align themselves with You."

Mother Oaks
Stand Strong

Dorothy Phillips was orphaned twice as a child, and the aunt who adopted her after her grandparents died passed away after Dorothy became an adult. She has overcome many obstacles and has been blessed with three sons and six grandchildren.

"As an adult looking back on all that happened, I realize I am blessed that I never felt like an orphan. I lived with my grandparents and found the love and care I needed there. Then I moved to my aunt's house where I felt loved. Things happen for a reason, and I believe if things had not happened as they did, I would not be as blessed as I am."

Even Weeping
Willows Smile

My sister, Carol Newborn, often volunteered in her granddaughter Nicole's first-grade classroom. She enjoyed the work and especially liked that Nicole had taught the entire class to call her "Mam-Maw."

Notes

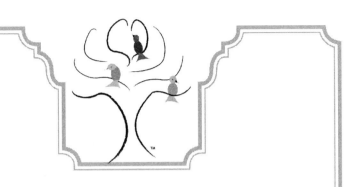

Chapter
4

A mother's heart is like the heart of a

mother bird who weaves her nest:

both have faith that their home will help

them raise their family and will satisfy

their maternal instincts.

This poem is about a mother bird whose faith helped her overcome unusual circumstances:

Metal Nest

Determined was the mother bird who
    built her nest of metal scraps,
The closest thing to twigs that she could find
    in city streets.

Wires, cords, snips of tin, woven painfully
    into a round home
Not exactly fit for her offspring but better
    than a bare ledge.

Workmen found the empty nest and
    carried it to one who knows birds.
Built by a resilient mother finch, he said.

I winced at the picture of the nest
    in a newspaper,
But as I looked I smiled about what
    all mothers know by instinct —

That the most vital building material is
    a shredded fabric lining.
A bit of softness is for baby birds and
    even the most tenacious mother.

When we mothers hold newborns, we dream about the future. We have faith that the child will grow up to be handsome, talented, and successful. Such were my thoughts when I recently bonded with my second granddaughter—a three-week-old newborn. As I comforted her after a crying spell, I held her over my heart and snuggled her up against my neck. I felt her breath. I smelled her lotion. The more I hugged her, the more she seemed to snuggle against me. At that moment, I was feeling more than the sensuality of holding a newborn: I felt the force of faith. I knew by faith that her parents would love her. I believed she would have a happy childhood and a wholesome life. I believed that God would embrace her and be with her all of her life and that she would love Him in return.

"Press toward the mark for the prize of the high calling of God in Christ Jesus."

— Philippians 3:12-14

Faith is one of the few true realities. It is greater than the circumstances my granddaughter will face in her life; for I know she will experience hardships, pain, and struggles. Overall, though, my faith in God, society, and parental love will carry her through this life and into the next one. I have woven a symbolic "nest of faith" for each of my children and grandchildren — most Christian mothers do. I will continue weaving my commitment of faith, hoping that my children and I will become the loving people God wants us to be in spite of our weaknesses, our circumstances, and the realities of the world.

The Bible tells about Jesus utilizing faith in Matthew 21:18 when He made His triumphal entry into Jerusalem. He healed many who came to him, and He banished the moneychangers from the temple. Both were powerful acts. Jesus' next act, though, seems shocking. He approached a fruitless fig tree in Matthew 21:19 and said, "Let no fruit grow on thee ... forever!" The tree withered and died — a huge force exerted for such a seemingly small reason. Jesus' next words show the kind of power that backed up His words. In verses 21 and 22, He says, "If ye have faith, and doubt not, ye shall not only do this which is done to the fig tree, but also if ye shall say unto this mountain, Be thou removed, and be thou cast into the sea; it shall be done. And all things, whatsoever ye shall ask in prayer, believing, ye shall receive."

Notice Jesus didn't say that God would answer our petitions of faith in the time frame we desire.

I have noticed in my own life that God often waited to answer my prayers when I began living, talking, and acting in certain ways. I have learned to ask the following petition quickly during adverse times, "Heavenly Father, what do You want me to learn?" and "Please help me learn my lessons quickly." My prayer related to my adult children is that my desire to influence them for Christ begins with me. I know that God wants me to become who I should be so Christ can work through me.

We read in Philippians 3:12-14 how Paul uses faith in his life. He reaches for perfection, knowing it will not be attainable, but in the process of forgetting the past and striving for perfection he is able to "press toward the mark for the prize of the high calling of God in Christ Jesus."

Mothers should apply that same attitude of forgetting the past and striving toward perfection. If and when we can achieve that attitude, we should be able to encourage our children for Christ no matter their age, and we can effectively encourage others. Think of all the words of encouragement Paul was able to write, and think of the countless lives his words have influenced. We, like Paul, must be patient and not give up on our hopes and dreams for our children, even if it takes years for God to answer our prayers for them. In fact, He may not even answer our prayers for our children until after we are in heaven.

We, like Paul, must be patient and not give up on our hopes and dreams for our children, even if it takes years for God to answer our prayers.

I discovered rather late in my child-rearing days a form of discipline using faith. Instead of being critical of my children, I learned to keep in mind the attitude that "I have faith that you will do the right thing," or "I have faith that you will be the best person you can be." I learned that these words are a great starting point when correcting children of all ages. In fact, the words don't sound like criticism at all, but instead they sound like encouragement, which they are.

Paul often felt inadequate to take the gospel to the world. Paul said that as a human he could not carry out God's command, but that God working through him could accomplish the task.

By the same token, if we as Christian mothers view our children's overwhelming problems and our inadequacies as barriers, we will fear failure. Our fears will make us unfit to encourage others, and we will miss out on opportunities to influence them for Christ. In Ephesians 2:10, Paul said, "For we are his workmanship, created in Christ Jesus unto good works, which God hath before ordained that we should walk in them." If God prepared us to do good works, then He will help us overcome our fears of doing good works.

> *"For we are his workmanship, created in Christ Jesus unto good works, which God hath before ordained that we should walk in them."*
> —*Ephesians 2:10*

A mother and son who set a good example of applying faith in family relationships is Mary and Jesus. In John 2:5, when Mary wants Jesus to turn water into wine, she says in faith about her son,

"Whatsoever he saith unto you, do it." Mary trusted, through faith, that Jesus would help her and others.

An example with which we can more closely identify is when Jesus appointed the disciple John to take care of his mother after He had been crucified. John 19:26,27 states, "When Jesus therefore saw his mother, and the disciple standing by, whom he loved, he saith unto his mother, Woman, behold thy son! Then saith he to the disciple, Behold thy mother! And from that hour that disciple took her unto his own home." Mary exercised faith in her son by accepting her new caregiver and bearing without protest her son's crucifixion. John, who took on a large responsibility, also believed that God through Christ could give him the blessings and the means to care for Mary.

Never underestimate faith. I often think back to the circumstances in my life that led me to becoming a Christian in an un-churched household. An elderly woman we called "Me-me" lived next door and was kind to our family during our difficult early life when we lived practically in poverty. She would come to our house and pay my mother fifty cents to roll her hair on bobby pins. As she sat at our kitchen table, we four girls would gather around and listen to her gentle stories about her family and her church. The tiny seed of faith from a woman I am convinced prayed for us has grown to become a giant tree that has produced Christians for three generations.

Scripture Readings and Prayers

1. Jesus found himself rocked by a storm that threatened not only his life but that of his loved ones.

❧ **Reading:** Matthew 8:26, " And he saith unto them, Why are ye fearful, O ye of little faith? Then he arose, and rebuked the winds and the sea; and there was a great calm."

❧ **Prayer:** "Dear Heavenly Father, as mothers and grandmothers, we will face storms even after our children are raised. Please give us great faith during these storms and give us great calm."

2. Jesus raised a widow's son.

❧ **Reading:** Luke 7:12-16. "Now when he came nigh to the gate of the city, behold, there was a dead man carried out, the only son of his mother, and she was a widow: and much people of the city was with her. And when the Lord saw her, he had compassion on her, and said unto her, Weep not. And he came and touched the bier: and they that bare him stood still. And he said, Young man, I say unto thee, Arise. And he that was dead sat up, and began to speak. And he delivered him to his mother. And there came a fear on all: and they glorified God, saying, that a great prophet is risen up among us; and, that God hath visited his people."

🕊 **Prayer:** "Dear Heavenly Father, we know that the age of miracles has passed, but you still have compassion on mothers and children. Protect us all and raise us up in faith to praise you."

3. Jesus said that His going to heaven would bring even greater assistance to our faith.

🕊 **Reading:** John 14:12-14. "I say unto you, He that believeth on me, the works that I do shall he do also; and greater works than these shall he do; because I go unto my Father. And whatsoever ye shall ask in my name, that will I do, that the Father may be glorified in the Son. If ye shall ask any thing in my name, I will do it."

🕊 **Prayer:** "Dear Heavenly Father, we ask you to allow the Holy Spirit to work through us and touch the lives of our children for Your name's sake. Call us to You and keep our hearts and our children's hearts as Yours for all eternity."

Mother Oaks
Stand Strong

Nancy Harrington left behind her children and grandchildren in Mesquite, Texas and moved with her husband Jim, who is minister at Greenbrier Church. They have worked hard to arrange one-on-one visits with each of their four grandchildren each year.

"My husband and I focus on each child during our visit. We play, share, talk, teach, study the Bible together, and pray. We listen to their problems. This one-on-one experience has been incredible. We've gotten to know each child in a more personal way. We hope we can continue these special visits well into their adult lives."

Even Weeping
Willows Smile

Greenbrier Church member Glenda Kirby gave her daughters-in-law a prayer and special letter she had written and dated to them when her sons were young. Daughter-in-law Kim calculated the date and time of the letter and figured it coincided exactly with the date and time of her 12th birthday party.

Notes

Chapter
5

A mother's heart is like a prism:

it can disperse the light of hope

and help her children discover

the array of colors within her heart.

I have felt amazingly fortunate twice in my life: I once saw a *glory* and, many years later, a *tangent arc*. A glory is a round rainbow at the top of the sky, and a tangent arc is an upside-down, rainbow arc above the sun.

One sunny day when my children were young, as I was hanging sheets on the clothesline, I looked up and saw the round rainbow. Later, I learned it was called a "glory" — a rare sight, I was told.

I had never seen a tangent arc in the atmosphere until 20 years later when I had grandchildren. One day, I was driving with them along I-20 from Atlanta to Anniston. I spotted another sight I had seen often — a pair of sundogs — bright, rainbow-like spots on each side of the sun. I looked above the sun where I had always wanted to see a tangent arc, and there it was — a mostly orange, upside down, partial rainbow. It lasted 45 minutes until I drove into a doughnut shop in Douglasville, Georgia. As dark approached, I stood in the parking lot and watched the arc disappear. Only then did the grandchildren and I go inside to select our doughnuts.

The dispersing of white light into colors is one of nature's greatest wonders. In the same way, a mother's heart receives the wonder of hope when she bonds with her child for the first time. She passes hope to the child, and she helps disperse that hope into talents, dreams, growth, beauty, and imagination. Ideally, a mother spends 18 years or so helping develop her child's characteristics so he or she can live happily and independently as an adult.

Mothers, no matter the ages of their children, should not lose the hope they discovered when giving birth to them, when raising them, or, later, when dealing with them as adult children. Mothers who maintain hope for their children's lives employ the same powerful force that God uses as He loves us throughout our entire lives and leads us to become the people He wants us to be. That love endures forever, even if at times we give Him reason to be disappointed in us.

My words cannot capture the story of Mary's and Elizabeth's hopes any better than the way the Bible tells the story beginning in Luke 1:35. As you read, try to feel the joy, especially considering that every Jewish woman wished to be the mother of the Christ child:

"And the angel answered and said unto her, The Holy Ghost shall come upon thee, and the power of the Highest shall overshadow thee: therefore also that holy thing which shall be born of thee shall be called the Son of God. And, behold, thy cousin Elisabeth, she hath also conceived a son in her old age: and this is the sixth month with her, who was called barren. For with God nothing shall be impossible. And Mary said, Behold the handmaid of the Lord; be it unto me according to thy word. And the angel departed from her.

And Mary arose in those days, and went into the hill country with haste, into a city of Juda; And entered into the house of Zacharias, and saluted Elisabeth. And it came to pass, that, when Elisabeth heard the salutation of Mary, the babe leaped in her womb; and Elisabeth was filled with the Holy Ghost: And she spake out with a loud voice, and said, Blessed art thou among women, and blessed is the fruit of thy womb. And whence is this to me, that the mother of my Lord should come to me? For, lo, as soon as the voice of thy salutation sounded in mine ears, the babe leaped in my womb for joy. And blessed is she that believed: for there shall be a performance of those things which were told her from the Lord. And Mary said, My soul doth magnify the Lord, And my spirit hath rejoiced in God my Saviour. For he hath regarded the low estate of his handmaiden: for, behold, from henceforth all generations shall call me blessed. For he that is mighty hath done to me great things; and holy is his name. And his mercy is on them that fear him from generation to generation. He hath shewed strength with his arm; he hath scattered the proud in the imagination of their hearts. He hath put down the mighty from their seats, and exalted them of low degree. He hath filled the hungry with good things; and the rich he hath sent empty away. He hath holpen his servant Israel, in remembrance of his mercy; As he spake to our fathers, to Abraham, and to his seed for ever. And Mary abode with her about three months, and returned to her own house."

We can imagine the joy these cousins shared because we remember how excited we were when expecting a child. We know what the Bible records of the later lives of Jesus and John the Baptist. The painful ending for both did not diminish the joy their mothers knew when carrying them and raising them. In the same way, modern mothers should maintain a hopeful attitude concerning their children's lives. We know our children will suffer from time to time, but we must not allow their pain or ours to diminish the joy of life itself. How can we remain hopeful in spite of the pain of earthly life?

Before answering that question, we should consider that modern mothers and children live longer than people in New Testament times. We maintain relationships with adult children much longer than the 18 years we are charged to raise them. Without undermining the importance of the childhood years, the adult years of children's lives should also be important to mothers, and worthy of all the hope and faith God can instill in mothers' hearts. How can mothers maintain this hope for 60, 70, even 80 years? The answer lies in the way a mother chooses to live. She should be a positive, hopeful

Christian who lives her life well in spite of difficulties. She should rely on God to fulfill her. Even mothers who were not Christians when raising their children can, after becoming Christians, implement the powers of faith, hope, and love when communicating and encouraging adult children, even if over long periods of time. To God, the element of time is not as much an issue as is obeying and applying his precepts.

Not only can mothers impact their children's lives after the children move away, but even after mothers die they can continue to impact their children's lives by the Christian way they lived and shared their love.

My husband has had a lifelong career as a funeral director. Many times during or after the funeral, he has heard adults make statements similar to the following about Christian mothers:

❖ "I never knew my mother's life touched so many other people."

❖ "The preacher summarized my mother's life well when he said she loved God."

❖ "I realized at my mother's funeral that I wanted to be more like her."

❖ "I looked around at my family members who were Christians, and realized I didn't want to live outside of God's love anymore."

No matter what the age of the child, a mother who prays for and encourages her child to live the Christian life can have an impact. God alone has the measuring tools for souls. We should never underestimate the result of even the smallest spiritual effort.

Another way of using a prism as a metaphor for instilling values in adult children is by thinking about the well-rounded Christian life. As light-filled Christians, God expects each of us to strive in five different aspects of life – spiritual, emotional, social, physical, and financial. We could compare these aspects to the five colors of the rainbow. All five aspects are areas we should pray for in our children's lives. Notice the ranking. Such are my preferences, though you may rank these aspects differently. Yet, spiritual life should be the first priority for all Christians (See Exodus 20:3 and Mark 12:30.).

How many of us Christian mothers encourage our young children and our adult children to excel in all other areas except the spiritual? I am guilty of this. I will call my adult children and ask about the family, the job, their friends, and how they are doing on a diet or a new workout regiment, etc. Less often, I ask about their spiritual lives.

Adults are not like children, though. They often consider their spiritual lives as private and may hesitate to discuss their relationship with God. As mothers, we do not want to be their conscience; nor do we want to appear as though we are forcing our spiritual beliefs on them, neither of which we can do.

There are other ways of encouraging our children spiritually, in addition to the obvious ones of kindness, prayerfulness, and positive living. We all give our children gifts for birthdays, for holidays, or for no occasion at all. We can give them gifts based on spiritual themes: a book, Christian music, tickets to a Christian-based seminar or concert, or we can donate money in their honor to a spiritual cause.

Living life on a spiritual level is perhaps one of the best ways to encourage our adult children.

Of course, all encouragement does not have to include money. Living life on a spiritual level is perhaps one of the best ways to encourage our adult children. Adult children are curious about the things we parents do, and they will notice sooner or later that spirituality is a priority for us. Adult children are curious about the ways their parents spend money. Spending our money on spiritual things to enhance our lives is another way of attracting our children's interest to spiritual matters.

One more way to seek God's influence in our children's lives is to ask other Christians to pray for them and to stay in touch with them after they leave home. Other people can influence our children sometimes when we are limited.

Scripture Readings and Prayers

1. During the first sermon Jesus preached, He told about the light of God.

   ❧ **Reading:** Matthew 4:16. "The people which sat in darkness saw great light; and to them which sat in the region and shadow of death light is sprung up."

   ❧ **Prayer:** "Dear Heavenly Father, fill us with the light of hope and help us to share that hope with our families and others."

2. **Reading:** Matthew 7:11,12. "If ye, then, being evil, know how to give good gifts unto your children, how much more shall your Father which is in heaven give good things to them that ask him?"

   ❧ **Prayer:** "Dear Heavenly Father, allow our gifts to our children to be used to glorify You, and allow the kindness and love we show to them also reflect the concern, care, and sensitivity that You show to us."

3. **Reading:** 1 Peter 3:1. The Bible says that husbands "may without the word be won by the conversation of the wives." It is only logical that a woman's godly example extends to others, too, including her children.

   ❧ **Prayer:** "Dear Heavenly Father, help us to focus on humbling ourselves before You, living the disciplined life You want us to live, and exalting You in everything we do."

Mother Oaks
Stand Strong

Helen Lackey trained her three children to carry out household duties after she began as a young mother to suffer from bi-polar disorder. She credits her husband, Bobby, her three children, and most of all, God, for keeping the family together in spite of her handicap.

"People I help who suffer from depression often ask what is going to happen to their children. I tell them that things happen to all families, and children can learn to understand what is happening, even when depression is involved. My family learned to emphasize the positive aspects of family life and to be thankful for my good days. Faith has always been a big part of our lives; yet, I have struggled with church members' reactions to my illness, which has sometimes been negative. Some didn't understand depression. A church needs to be educated about mental illness. That can make a big difference in how a person copes with depression."

Even Weeping
Willows Smile

"I was not in the best of moods during my recovery from childbirth. I remember one day Mother was chopping cabbage at the counter, and the noise was driving me crazy. I gave her such a hard look that she went out to the back deck to finish making coleslaw. A few days later, when she left and drove 250 miles back home, I cried for a long time. I couldn't help but wish I could hear her chopping that stupid cabbage." – Brianne Kughn Hendrick

❧ *Notes* ❧

Chapter
6

A mother's heart is like a

kaleidoscope — ever changing,

multi-faceted, and lovely on the inside.

She should expect new opportunities

after her children leave home,

opportunities that can lead her to a

colorful, bright future.

I bought my seven and five-year-old grandchildren a kaleidoscope that had an end cap. They could select whatever they wanted to fill it. We had a great time finding pretty rocks, bits of glass, some glow-in-the-dark plastic bits, and a snip of a red drinking straw. We looked through the tube for a while at all the possible views those items made; then we dumped them out and looked for more. We found marbles, colored wire, food color lids, and many things to make other scenes. They tired of the toy after a few days, but I laid it on my desk and thought of the possibilities.

Like our experience with that particular kaleidoscope, a mother can explore the contents of her heart to make sure it is filled with beautiful and bright characteristics. Philippians 4:8 says that whatever is honest, just, pure, lovely, virtuous, praiseworthy, and of good report – "think on these things."

A Christian mother's mind is an avenue to her heart, so whatever she "places" in her mind is what her heart absorbs. A mother who was raised in the church from childhood was taught this concept when young, and when one is young it is easy to be idealistic.

As we age, we sometimes allow our hearts to grow crusty with life's disappointments, hardships, and pains. Often, we longtime, faithful Christians do not even realize how rigid our hearts have become. After all, we have stayed faithful to our church, we have prayed for years, we have read and continue to read our Bibles, we try to do everything we know to be "right," but have our hearts grown hard with respect to our children?

What disappointments have we mothers faced in dealing with our children?

One way to keep our heart soft as it relates to our children is to face and resolve our disappointments. One morning in my ladies' Sunday school class, the teacher asked us who we would choose to hold the end of the rope if we were dangling over a cliff. One mother made us all laugh when she said, "not my children." The remark stayed with me, though. What disappointments have we mothers faced in dealing with our children? We gave them life. We worked for them and sacrificed for them. We hurt when they hurt and laughed when they laughed. As we age, we sometimes ask ourselves other questions:

❖ Do our children not owe us mothers a great debt?
❖ Should they not provide us with companionship?
❖ Can they not come to see us more often?
❖ Can they not help us more?
❖ Will they place us in a nursing facility when our health fails?

The Bible provides some answers for our deepest concerns.

The stories of Joseph and Jacob provide us with a look into the ways the elderly were to be treated by God's people in the Old Testament. After Joseph was reunited with his brothers, Jacob was brought to him. By then, Jacob was poverty-stricken because of a drought, and he was depressed because he thought Joseph had died years earlier. Joseph learned of his father's circumstances, and he did what he could do to help him. He did not relinquish his duties as a leader in Pharaoh's court. Instead, he provided care indirectly for his father. He gave him a place to live and food to eat, and he allowed his brothers to continue providing Jacob's day-to-day care as they had always done.

In spite of his responsibilities, Joseph maintained the utmost respect for his father. Out of his abundance, Joseph made certain his father had sustenance and respect. Jacob's response provides us with a good example, too. Nowhere do we read that Jacob expected Joseph to provide direct care. Nowhere do we read that he complained that his care was inadequate; though we do know that his heart longed to be back in the land of his fathers, a simple request we often hear from old people — they just want to go home. So what did Joseph and his brothers do? They respected their father enough to carry out his request after he died. Likewise, each modern generation should work together to provide and receive care and to honor each other in love.

The New Testament provides a similar example for parents and adult children. The story of Jesus and Mary provides us with a glimpse into the ways the elderly were to be treated by God's people in the New Testament. As He was dying, Jesus presented John and Mary to each other. In John 19:26,27, the Bible says, "When Jesus therefore saw his mother, and the disciple standing by, whom he loved, he saith unto his mother, Woman, behold thy son! Then saith he to the disciple, Behold thy mother! And from that hour that disciple took her unto his own home." Jesus knew by John's cooperation that His mother would have a place to live and food to eat, and He showed her great respect. Jesus, even though He had no earthly abundance, still made certain His mother had sustenance before He died. Nowhere do we read that Mary expected Jesus to provide direct care. Nowhere do we read of her complaining that the care was inadequate.

We gain strength when we learn that our faith and joy can raise us above our circumstances.

These two examples give us many answers to the problems facing the elderly and middle-aged generations in the years to come. God's younger generation of adult children should make certain their parents are sustained and respected. God's older generation of parents should make certain they submit to the care their adult children can provide. Each individual family must address the details of the circumstances surrounding the provision of care for the elderly. God does not expect the younger generation to give up the duties they have toward their jobs and immediate families to care for their elderly parents, but God does expect the care to be respectful. It is also the family's responsibility to balance out what is emotionally and physically healthy for all who are involved.

A mother's responsibility toward her children changes with each stage of life. Like brilliant colors in a kaleidoscope, her heart can portray beauty in the many ways her duties change through the years. Kaleidoscopes spread their beauty in different mediums – light, oil, and air. Some kaleidoscopes have rare gems inside. Others are made with lowly materials. Kaleidoscopes come in all different shapes and sizes. Some are made like bottles, tables, tubes, and boxes. The Kaatskill Kaleidoscope in Mount Tremper, New York is even made out of a silo! A mother's heart is like a kaleidoscope in many ways, but most important is the beauty it reflects throughout her life in the lives of her children.

A mother's responsibility toward her children changes with each stage of life.

A woman as a daughter must deal with issues that her adult children will possibly face with her. The Golden Rule should apply: if we "do unto" our parents as we hope our children "do unto" us, then God will be pleased. He promised in 1 Corinthians 10:13 that he would never put more on us than we could bear. The proof of this truth lies in the fact that we are still alive physically, emotionally, and spiritually, even though we, at our mature age, have probably dealt with hardships far worse than what we thought we could endure. God knew differently, though, didn't He? When we look back over our lives, the hardships we have endured have strengthened us, taught us, and increased our faith.

God says in Nehemiah 8:10 "the joy of the Lord is your strength." Think about that. When we as Christian women focus on Jesus, when we draw our happiness from the truth that He lives in our hearts, then we will not be bound by hardships. In fact, when we learn that our faith and joy can raise us above our circumstances, we gain strength. When we learn that we can be happy for no other reason than that Jesus lives in our hearts each moment and that He sustains us by His blessings, we gain strength. Indeed, our "joy" in the Lord is our "strength."

Scripture Readings and Prayers

1. The love Jacob and Joseph shared for one another reveals the deep bond between the two even though they never lived together as adults.

🕊 **Reading**: Genesis 48:11. Jacob said, "I had not thought to see thy face: and, lo, God hath shewed me also thy seed." The Bible says in verse 12 that Joseph "bowed himself with his face to the earth" before Jacob.

🕊 **Prayer**: "Dear Heavenly Father, no matter what our circumstances, allow us to preserve the great love and respect toward one another that Jacob and Joseph shared."

2. In the 2004 movie, The Passion of Christ, the focus on Mary's lack of interference along with her support and love in Jesus' life and death gives us a visual example of selfless love.

🕊 **Reading**: Mark 15:47 and Acts 1:14 show us that Mary was nearby during the time of Jesus's death and resurrection.

🕊 **Prayer**: "Dear Heavenly Father, help us maintain the same faith, hope, and love for our children as Mary maintained throughout Jesus' life."

3. Worry about "what will happen to me" causes many problems for older mothers: anxiety, depression, and health disorders. Christian women should take every precaution possible to provide for themselves and then focus on God's provisions.

🕊 **Reading**: Luke 12:27. "Consider the lilies how they grow: they toil not, they spin not; and yet I say unto you, that Solomon in all his glory was not arrayed like one of these."

🕊 **Prayer**: "Dear Heavenly Father, please let us cast our cares upon You and not upon our children."

Mother Oaks
Stand Strong

Jane Blackwood is a mother who raised her biological children Angela and Brad, as well as her adopted son Shannon who was blinded at infancy. Angela has also adopted a special-needs child Hannah, and is raising her along with her other children.

"Giving birth to children and watching them develop and blossom only 'spurs you on' to reach out to a precious child who has no loving mother. Having a special child in our family taught us more lessons about God and love than any other single thing in our lives."

Even Weeping
Willows Smile

The night before my son Jeremy and daughter-in-law Jennifer married, Jennifer's mother, Patty Manning, admitted to slipping into Jennifer's bedroom to watch her sleep: "just one more time," she said.   — The Author

❧ *Notes* ❧

Chapter
7

A mother's heart is like an Etch A
Sketch®: a few upside-down shakes and
drawing can begin anew.

Hope lies in the fact that we may give and receive forgiveness from our children and thus improve our relationships. A Christian mother knows when she has made mistakes, even if only in hindsight. She learns, too, that sometimes benefits are gained from admitting those mistakes.

A common complaint teen-agers and college students make about their parents is that parents never admit they are wrong. This type of attitude sends children the message that they, too, should never admit mistakes. These attitudes can create an impasse between children and their parents. God's Word, though, teaches that mistakes should be acknowledged and that repentance should take place.

One of the problems mothers face is that we are programmed into being role models. Even though children do not know it when they are small, we wing our way along as we raise them. We are by nature teachers, and most of us make a deliberate effort to be good teachers. Why, then, do we fail to admit our weaknesses to our children as we raise them, and why do we look back and dwell on past mistakes? We have too much pride to admit our errors.

Probably the lowest point during my years of raising children was a day when I was in a hurry to straighten the house. I walked into the bathroom my children shared.

The toilet was covered with dried streaks of bright pink nail polish. I fumed that my daughter, the only one I thought could have made the mess, had neither tried to wipe it up nor tell me about it. About that time, she walked into the bathroom.

"Why did you do this?" I asked her.

"I didn't," she said too quickly to convince me that she was telling me the truth.

We should smother out the sins in others by confronting wrong with love, by resolving our difficulties, and then by continuing relationships, also in love.

I slapped her across the face. I will never forget the look in her eyes — total betrayal. I almost cry (and cry even as I write this) every time I think back on that awful memory. She turned and walked out of the bathroom. I sank to my knees and starting dabbing at the pink polish with a tissue — not knowing what else to do. Not two minutes later, one of my sons walked by. "Mom, I meant to tell you about that mess I made," he said.

I was too upset to ask him what he had been doing with the polish. I got up from the bathroom floor, found my daughter, and begged her forgiveness. She was crying, and I began crying. Since that time, I have tried to use the moment as a touchstone to never allow myself to be that mean or to jump to conclusions. Then and there, I made up my mind to apologize quickly whenever I failed as a mother. I remember a few years later telling one of my sons I was sorry about something that had happened – I don't even remember what. He reached over and hugged me.

"All my friends can't believe I have a mother who apologizes," he said. (I was flattered. We mothers take our victories where we can.)

The Apostle Paul is a great example of a person with an Etch-A-Sketch® heart. His relationship with Barnabas is an example of his attitude toward forgiveness. Paul and Barnabas traveled together from Antioch to many places as they taught new Christians. Eventually, they disagreed about which routes to take, and the Bible tells us in Acts 15:39: "And the contention was so sharp between them, that they departed asunder one from the other." Later, the Bible in Galatians 2:13 says that Barnabas was led astray from the Christian life. Paul did not forget Barnabas, though, and in Colossians 4:10 said that if the other disciples saw Barnabas to "receive him."

We need to strive to be like Paul, courageous, forgiving, and quick to continue in loving relationships.

One of the reasons for the disagreement between Paul and Barnabas was John Mark. Acts 15:38 tells us that John Mark had deserted them in Pamphylia, and Paul was not happy when Barnabas insisted on taking

John Mark along on a subsequent mission. Years after the separation between Paul and Barnabas, Paul had obviously resolved his issues with John Mark. He wrote to Timothy, as recorded in 2 Timothy 4:11: "Take Mark, and bring him with thee: for he is profitable to me for the ministry."

Paul also had disagreements with Peter. In Galatians 2:14, Paul confronted Peter for teaching the Gentiles that circumcision was necessary. Paul corrected Peter before others for not teaching that our salvation is in Christ alone. (The same issue led Barnabas astray.) We know through their writings in the New Testament that both Paul and Peter continued on the same mission of teaching new Christians.

Peter was quick to confront issues and quick to forgive. In 1 Peter 4:8, he said, "for charity shall cover the multitude of sins. Use hospitality one to another without grudging."

The word cover in Greek means *smother*. The dual meaning allows Christians to understand we should *smother out* the sins in others by confronting wrong with love, by resolving our difficulties, and then by continuing relationships, also in love.

Paul confirmed his belief for the idea when he wrote in Colossians 3:13,14: "Forbearing one another, and forgiving one another, if any man have a quarrel against any: even as Christ forgave you, so also do ye. And above all these things put on charity, which is the bond of perfectness."

Our children appreciate a humble and forgiving spirit. They may not always understand why parents make mistakes, but usually they are quick to forgive. Children identify with parents who make mistakes.

They are quicker to open up about their own

The hope of forgiveness allows adult children to emotionally dwell near us, and it allows us to tear down walls of power we erected as we raised them.

mistakes, and, when their confessions are handled in love, children learn to ask their parents for guidance sometimes even before mistakes are made.

We need to strive to be like Paul, courageous, forgiving, and quick to continue in loving relationships. Embracing these three attitudes leads toward resolution of our past mistakes and the possibility of a deeper communication with God and others in the future.

Mothers who want to build a bridge to estranged children should take the initiative to bridge the gap by admitting past mistakes.

I had a call this week from a 35-year-old friend who was stricken with grief over the death of her father. Right before his death, he had taken the initiative to call her after years of alienation due to his alcoholism. He told her in his conversation that he realized his mistakes had hurt her. Not too long afterward, he died. As hard as her grief is, she would have suffered worse if her father had never reached out to her. She will grieve for a while, but accepting her father's repentance will help her heal.

The Bible tells us to repent because godly sorrow brings about good, whereas society tells us not to repent because sorrow is viewed as weakness.

The hope of forgiveness allows adult children to emotionally dwell near us, and it allows us to tear down walls of power we erected as we raised them. Christian mothers with Etch-A-Sketch® hearts should be quick to see mistakes. We should be ready to give our hearts a shake to start anew as often as necessary.

Scripture Readings and Prayers

1. Love and peace should be the goal in our families, not mistrust and resentment over past mistakes.

❧ **Reading:** 2 Corinthians 13:11. "Be perfect, be of good comfort, be of one mind, live in peace; and the God of love and peace shall be with you."

❧ **Prayer:** "Dear Heavenly Father, help us as mature mothers to humble ourselves and allow us to maintain hope for stronger relationships."

2. **Reading:** 2 Corinthians 7:10. "For godly sorrow worketh repentance to salvation ... but the sorrow of the world worketh death."

❧ **Prayer:** "Dear Heavenly Father, allow us to recognize that the difference in these two types of sorrow is You, and help us have the godly sorrow and repentance that benefits You, our children, and us."

3. According to the introductory passages of Corinthians in the Dickson Bible, Jesus' brother James did not understand Jesus' importance until after His resurrection. After the resurrection, however, James became a devout Christian and church leader (1306).

❧ **Reading:** James 5:16. "Confess your faults one to another, and pray one for another, that ye may be healed. The effectual fervent prayer of a righteous man availeth much."

❧ **Prayer:** "Dear Heavenly Father, heal our relationships. Help us to realize how powerful and effective are our prayers for our children when we are in a righteous relationship with You."

Mother Oaks
Stand Strong

Yamileth Echevarria is a Spanish-speaking mother who left an adult daughter and two grandchildren in Panama to move to the United States with her younger daughter and her husband. They serve the Hispanic membership at the Greenbrier Church and travel as missionaries each year to Panama.

"The transition from Panama to the United States was a sweet and sour experience. The immigration bureaucracy prohibited my adult daughter and grandchildren from moving with us. Leaving them behind was the hardest part of moving. However, getting to know others in other Latin American cultures and being able to evangelize them is a great opportunity that I am thankful for."

Even Weeping
Willows Smile

"One time I drove 500 miles from Alabama to Indianapolis to pick up my older son, Jeremy. He had broken up with his girlfriend, had left college, and wanted to return home. After we packed his belongings, I returned indoors to see him with the saddest look on his face I'd ever seen: he was saying good-bye to his pet goldfish."

– Barry Kughn

Chapter
8

A mother's heart is like the heart of

a gardener: the hope she has for her

children's interest in spirituality,

like a gardener who plants a seed,

perseveres even though the results

are not always what she expects.

She controls what she can in the

garden of her heart.

I have experimented for many years with patio gardening. I give all of my plants a daily watering, plenty of fertilizer and insect spray, and I regularly prune dead stems. Even with this equal treatment, the same species of plants will behave in different ways.

Jesus speaks of this puzzle in Matthew 13:3-8 when He tells about the parable of the sower. Verses 18-23 explain how the soil represents each hearer's heart. The seed is God's message. The varied results show how differently each hearer receives the seed.

We Christian mothers hope that our children will have rich, fertile hearts for God's Word. We lose hope, though, when they seem to turn their backs on spiritual matters, and they allow the condition of their hearts to seemingly dry up. Instead of losing heart, though, we mothers should hope that life's experiences will serve as a cultivator for our children's hearts.

We should cultivate our hearts, too, and remember our own pasts. Our hearts have changed throughout the years. There were times when we have felt close to God and times when we did not. We have had positive and negative spiritual influences. The soil of our hearts has at times felt dry and hard, and at other times felt crowded with weeds. Most Christian mothers, thankfully, maintain tender and rich hearts.

We can most effectively influence our children for Christ when we control the elements that make our

hearts what they should be: good soil. There are several
ways to do this.

One way to keep the heart tender
and open toward God's Word is
through church attendance. We
should attend worship services
and Bible studies faithfully. In
fact, most Christian mothers know
the Bible commands attendance:
"Not forsaking the assembling of
ourselves together, as the manner of
some is; but exhorting one another,"
Hebrews 10:25.

One way to keep the heart tender and open toward God's Word is through church attendance. We should attend worship services and Bible studies faithfully.

Even the mother who attends every church service
cannot force church attendance on adult children. They
will refuse to discuss the matter if she "checks up" on
them, hints to them frequently, or badgers them about
their lack of attendance. There is nothing wrong, though,
with an occasional frank and positive conversation about
the importance of worshipping God regularly, when an
appropriate opportunity presents itself. Acts of respect,
though, are sometimes better than conversation.

My father was an abused child without a positive
male figure, a fact I learned when I was an older child. I
was old enough by then, too, to worry about my father's
soul if he died. I was a faithful Christian, and I wanted
him to be one. Yet, I felt helpless to talk to my father

about these things, so I did what I could: I obeyed him, I stayed faithful to my church, and I was careful to speak only about the positive traits of my church. Time passed, and I married and moved out of my father's home. I lived near my family, though, and continued to influence them the best I could. Before I realized it, years passed until a time when my husband, recovering from back surgery, and my young children and I moved into another house. My father told me to hire some men to help us move. "I don't need to," I told him. "The friends from our congregation will help us." My father shook his head and said no one would show up. We moved the following Saturday.

Nineteen men drove up in several cars and trucks (one with a trailer bed). Within four hours, they had loaded and unloaded our belongings and had set our furniture in place in the new house. My father called me that night and said, "We'll be at church services in the morning. I want to be a part of a church where people help each other like that."

We contribute toward the development of a soft, pliable environment when we speak kind words to our adult children and have fellowship with them.

My father, who had already mellowed with age, became the most enthusiastic Christian I had ever seen during the next few years. He made friends at church, was faithful to attend services, and served other church members. My father faced surgery not many years after his conversion. He told us that God's peace was in his heart. My father never awoke from the surgery, and later I was more thankful for his conversion than sad for my loss. My twenty-year prayer for my father to become a faithful Christian became a reality because God sought him and encouraged him through me.

Good soil is soft, rich, and located in an area that is not too dry, too wet, or too cold. We contribute toward the development of a soft, pliable environment when we speak kind words to our adult children and have fellowship with them. We enrich their hearts when we encourage them toward wholesome experiences. We pave a path for them to learn about God when we communicate with them in kindness.

Other ways of maintaining and enriching the conditions of our own hearts are prayer, Bible study, meditation, thanksgiving, music, and reading.

One issue that does not change very much in family life is that adult children want to know that they are as beloved by their parents as are their siblings. As mothers, we foster good feelings within the family when we spend money equally on our adult children and grandchildren. We foster good feelings when we divide our time as equally as we can, and we strengthen the family when we control the words we use in criticism toward our adult children, grandchildren, and in-laws.

Equal treatment toward our children should not stop after they leave home, even though then it is sometimes a harder struggle. Some adult children, by their nature, communicate more with their parents. Some struggle with life on various levels, and some accept help from their parents, whereas others do not. Too, the personalities of children and parents change over time, which alters feelings (especially when in-laws are part of the equation).

One of the most important ways we help our adult children is by putting God first in our own lives.

Paul speaks about the ideal type of conversation in Colossians 4:6 when he says that it should be "always with grace" and "seasoned with salt." Conversation full of grace, esteem, favor, and kindness enhances relationships as salt enhances food. Salt, like kind words, both preserves and improves.

One of the most important ways we help our adult children is by putting God first in our own lives. I worried when my children were young and cherubic that I loved them even more than I loved God. Their beauty astonished me, and my heart was wrapped up in theirs to the point where I wondered sometimes if I loved them too much.

My attachment to the children began loosening, of course, during the teen years (what parent's feelings are not challenged then?). The challenge of raising teen-agers became so great that I had no choice as a Christian but to turn their care over to God. Those were the years when I learned what the gardener learns: it is sometimes necessary to allow God to take over in areas where we cannot. The flowers either blossom or they do not. Sometimes a flower the gardener tosses takes root in other soil and thrives, and sometimes a flower given up for dead presses up through the soil the following Spring. We should never throw up our hands and walk away from our children when we can maintain hope and expect rejuvenation.

Paul writes in Colossians 4:2 that his followers should devote themselves to "prayer, and watch in the same with thanksgiving."

Are we Christian mothers always thankful, or do we sometimes sink into despair when we think we have failed as mothers? Thankfulness, like joy, raises us up to a higher level of living. Thankfulness improves our attitude, our outlook, and our influence upon others. No matter what circumstances send us into the valley of despair, we should climb out along the banks of thankfulness.

Like a gardener who maintains the tools and grooms the garden, a mother with hope in her heart for her children will do whatever is effective and appropriate to maintain hope that her children's souls will blossom in God's time.

Scripture Readings and Prayers

1. The most effective mothers discipline their small children by stating the desired behavior: "I know what a good little boy or girl you are and that you won't lie any more. I want you to think about that as you sit in this corner chair." This type of discipline places a hopeful spin on the transgression and is effective even with adult children, (even if they are too old to sit in the corner).

   Reading: Philippians 1:19-28 demonstrates this principle of positive expectation.

   Prayer: "Dear Heavenly Father, help us believe that the good seeds we planted in our children's hearts when they were young will yield fruit."

2. Paul was a parental figure to Timothy. In 1 Timothy 4:1-5, Paul lists the bad things people will do to pervert Christ's teachings and tells how he disciplined in a positive way.

   Reading: 1 Timothy 4:6. "If thou put the brethren in remembrance of these things, thou shalt be a good minister of Jesus Christ, nourished up in the words of faith and of good doctrine, whereunto thou hast attained."

🕊 **Prayer:** "Dear Heavenly Father, help us to be good ministers for Jesus and to nourish others with encouraging and holy words."

3. Helen Keller once wrote, "If I am happy in spite of my deprivations, if my happiness is so deep that it is a faith, so thoughtful that it becomes a philosophy of life, — if, in short, I am an optimist, my testimony to the creed of optimism is worth hearing." Quote from the essay on "Optimism" (1903).

🕊 **Reading:** 1 Peter 1:8 tells how we may have joy because we believe in Jesus.

🕊 **Prayer:** "Dear Heavenly Father, no matter our handicaps in life, help us to have unspeakable joy just because Jesus lives and that He lives in us."

It is sometimes necessary to allow God to take over in areas where we cannot.

Mother Oaks Stand Strong

Lynn Luke raised two children and then provided daycare for her three grandchildren. The last grandchild, Isaac, weighed only one pound, seven ounces when born and required special care for several months. Lynn has had to reduce the amount of daycare she could provide because she developed breast cancer and was undergoing treatments.

"I always enjoyed being a mother, and being a grandmother has been even more fun. God blessed us through Isaac, who has overcome many obstacles during his first few years. The other two grandchildren, Derrick and Tessa, as young as they are, have been so supportive and loving to me during my illness. I've been thankful not only for my flesh and blood family but also for my church family. They have been here for me."

Even Weeping Willows Smile

I called my five-year-old granddaughter Taylor on the telephone one afternoon and asked to speak to her mother, who is my daughter-in-law. "Mommy," she said, "Your husband's mother is on the phone."

— The Author

🖋 *Notes* 🖋

Chapter
9

In Christ, a mother's heart

is like white linen:

it is pure and resilient when she allows

God's love to live there.

My mother is known as the stain buster. All of her children and grandchildren bring their stained garments to her, and she usually removes the stains without a trace. Last summer, I presented her with an impossible challenge: the heirloom, linen dress my granddaughter wore in a wedding. It was stained with chocolate and was accidentally left in a hot car for several days. After bleaching it three times, I took the dress to my mother. She tried several of her favorite products, including dye remover. "The stain is permanent," she said. "Even I can't get it out." I did not take her word.

Sin will stain a heart to the point that its basic structure is changed.

I searched on the Internet until I learned that some fibers develop an altered structure when badly stained. Thankfully, my granddaughter's dress was lightened enough for us to have some photographs made by folding the dark spots away from the camera. Mother was right, though: no one could get out the stain.

The human heart without God is like altered fabric. Sin will stain a heart to the point that its basic structure is changed. Sins stain relationships, too, as we know all too well. Our relationships with our children are altered when either one of us sins.

Most mothers, by way of forgiveness, restore altered relationships. The problem is that love often impairs judgment. Many mothers forgive so easily that they fail to allow adult children to learn from mistakes.

In Luke 15:11-31, Jesus tells the familiar story of the prodigal son. We can learn some not-so-familiar lessons, though, from what the father did not do. He did not leave his house and search for the son who had taken his inheritance and squandered it. The Bible does not indicate that the father sent anyone to spy on or to exhort the son. The father appeared to allow the son to sin, to learn life's hard lessons, and to make up his own mind about returning. The Bible indicates that the father had forgiven the son before he had even asked for forgiveness. Verse 20 says, "But when he was yet a great way off, his father saw him, and had compassion, and ran, and fell on his neck, and kissed him." The Bible also indicates that the father took action to forgive his son. He ordered the son a robe, a ring, and sandals. Next the father ordered a fine meal in celebration of his son's return. We mothers identify with this desire to shower gifts on returning children.

There is one other thing, however, the father did not do that sometimes we are tempted to do. The father did not restore to the prodigal son the riches that had been spent. Instead, verse 31 says that "all" the father had he gave to the older son. Like the altered fabric in the dress, the altered relationship between the father and the prodigal son meant the son lost his inheritance. This action allowed the son to learn lessons of humility and gratitude toward his father.

Once, from the corner of my eye, I watched a family at a restaurant. Two preteen daughters bickered at the table after what appeared to have been a pleasant evening dinner. The mother gave them an exasperated look but softly said, "Just forget the hot chocolate that you ordered." When the waitress brought out two mugs filled with hot chocolate and piled with whipped cream, the mother allowed her to set the mugs before the children. "I wonder if she allows them to drink it," I thought. When the waitress walked away, the mother discreetly removed the hot chocolate from before the girls, gave one mug to her husband and set the other down for herself. Without a word, the girls sat and watched as their parents consumed their hot chocolates. Their faces showed that they were learning one of life's tough lessons — do not argue in front of Mother at the table, at least until after dessert is served. Sadly, too many of us mothers (and soft-hearted fathers) would have relented and allowed the children to drink the chocolate.

We mature mothers know that God does not relent when teaching us life's lessons, but we have trouble allowing Him to teach our children. Perhaps God allows us and our adult children to struggle with life's hardships in order to remove impurities from our hearts. He wants our hearts to be like new, white linen, and He wants us to be submissive when He deals with us. Yes, God is the only being who is better at getting out stains than my mother.

The finest heart comes from a godly life and costs much in terms of time, patience, and continual striving.

I do not have enough space in this study to fully develop the exception to this rule of allowing adult children to learn on their own, which is when they are involved with drugs, alcohol, and abusive relationships. I believe help should be sought at those times. In these cases, the mature parents should consult counselors, if for no other reason than the professionals can help the parents cope with what has happened. Professionals can also teach mature mothers how to give their adult children effective emotional, psychological, and social support.

Stains are not the only similarities between fine linen and the heart:

❖ Linen is strong like the loving heart. It is made from two-foot long fibers of the flax plant. When the fiber is removed, it is folded during processing to strengthen the fabric.

❖ Linen's endurance is legendary as is the heart of a loving mother. Linen has been found intact in the tombs of many ancient ruins. One of the most famous pieces is the Shroud of Turin, believed by some to be the actual fabric that wrapped Jesus' body. Scientists have studied whether the fibers of the shroud were altered with energy released when Jesus' spirit was resurrected. We will likely never know for sure on earth, but the theory attests to the resilience of the fabric.

❖ Pure, fine linen is highly prized, as is a loving heart. The finest heart comes from a godly life and costs much in terms of time, patience, and continual striving.

Proverbs 31:26 describes the ideal mother as being one who "openeth her mouth with wisdom; and in her tongue is the law of kindness."

❖ Fine linen is lovely, full of sheen, texture, and movement; and it is often used for garments worn on special occasions. The pure heart is lovely, too, and shines through the godly heart for others to see and enjoy.

Proverbs 31:26 describes the ideal mother as being one who "openeth her mouth with wisdom; and in her tongue is the law of kindness." Perhaps we mothers were not always "ideal" when raising our children. We probably did not always use perfect wisdom, and sometimes we were caught up in moments of stress and anguish. Most likely we sometimes said wrong things, and thankfully most of us said many things right as well. Now that the children are out of the home, most of us are less stressed. We have more control over our words and our actions, and maybe now is the time to focus on becoming more ideal.

A word here to mature parents raising grandchildren: You are to be commended for the sacrifice you make. Surely God will reward you richly.

There is one more area where mature mothers should be more ideal: dealing with our children's spouses. It is easy for us to displace our frustration with our adult children by blaming their spouses. However, mothers learn quickly that misplaced frustration toward our children's spouses usually backfires. Not only does blaming the in-laws alter our relationship with them, but also our children will resent us for having a negative attitude toward their spouses. Mothers who get in the middle of disagreements between their children and their children's spouses often find themselves out in the cold.

Like fine linen, mature Christian mothers should age gracefully and grow in ideal Christian behavior.

Scripture Readings and Prayers

1. **Reading:** Luke 15:17. From the story of the prodigal son in Luke 15, consider verse 17 when the Bible says the son "came to himself." Consider the son's characteristics that led up to his decision.

    ❦ **Prayer:** "Dear Heavenly Father, give us mothers the wisdom to allow our children to learn from their mistakes, and protect them while they are learning from life's hardships, as You protected us."

2. **Reading**: Luke 15: 28-31. In Luke 15, the father counsels the elder son in verses 28-31. His behavior was opposite from his younger brother's; yet, he was in need of his father's instruction, too.

🕊 **Prayer:** "Dear Heavenly Father, give us mothers the wisdom of the ages; so we can effectively know what to say and what to do to encourage our children toward godliness."

3. **Reading**: Proverbs 31:30. "[A] woman that feareth the Lord, she shall be praised. Give her of the fruit of her hands; and let her own works praise her in the gates." Modern Christian mothers are also worthy of the fruits they have earned and are worthy of the praise they receive.

🕊 **Prayer:** "Dear Heavenly Father, thank you that Your spirit in us allows us to have a heart of love for our families and for others."

Mother Oaks
Stand Strong

Nancy Morrow is one of the church secretaries at Greenbrier Church, and she is the daughter of a mother suffering from Alzheimer's. Nancy's son, Corey, has given her the blessing of two grandchildren."

"I loved my mother, but I lost her when the disease took over. It's a horrible, devastating disease. It was hard on us as a family to remember the lively person she had always been. My family throughout the years had always taken care of various relatives with different diseases, but this was different. It was heartbreaking for us to hear Mother cry and not to know what was wrong. I visited her, and I was glad she had excellent care, but this was really hard."

Even Weeping
Willows Smile

Diana Ockay was babysitting her three-year-old granddaughter Kinsley one day when she learned how often Kinsley's family must have been eating out at fast food restaurants. Diana prepared some vegetables and meat on a special plate for Kinsley, and she rolled the same up in a soft taco shell for herself and her husband. Kinsley sat down at the table, took a look at the difference in the servings, and she said, "I want a Taco Bell, too."

Chapter
10

A mother's heart

is like the heart of a

tightrope walker: balanced,

discerning,

alert, and disciplined.

A loving heart carries with it the expectation of good things to come but knows that failure is the condition of the human spirit. A loving heart focuses on the good things, not the bad. Even mothers who have not implemented the principles of love in the past can employ them for the future.

A loving heart focuses on the good things, not the bad.

Love begets love. Once there was a disgruntled wife. She visited her minister and told him how terrible her husband was. "I despise him," she said. "I would leave him, but that is what he wants me to do. I want to stay with him and make him as miserable as he has made me."

The minister, a wise man, told the wife he knew of a way to achieve her goal. "First, I want you to be kind," he said. "I want you to speak sweet words to him, to prepare his favorite meals, to look your best when you are with him. Treat him this way for several weeks, and when you think he is accustomed to it, leave him. You'll break his heart, and he will be miserable." Several weeks went by, and the minister called the woman aside. "Have you left your husband yet?" he asked.

"Leave him?" she said. "Why, he's the kindest, sweetest man I've ever met – just the way I've always wanted him to be. Why would I leave him?"

The same love can be applied to adult children. Even mothers who may have behaved selfishly, gossiped about family members, prodded adult children to "go to" church and questioned everything adult children did with a critical spirit, even those mothers can change their speech and actions. Mature mothers who treat adult children with the utmost respect, kind words, pleasant conversation, and a positive tone can earn the same words and acts of love from their children.

A mother must also maintain a prayerful attitude about her children's problems and not view them through rose-colored glasses. A discerning mother should not be blinded by love but should see reality. Otherwise, her blindness will abet her children's selfish motivations and actions. Often when young children are living at home, the mother is involved in their lives and is directly or indirectly responsible for their success. Once the children leave home for college, these "new" adults often experience failure that is hard for mothers to acknowledge.

I remember swallowing this difficult pill. One of my children was a straight-A student in high school and won a scholarship that was almost cancelled by the end of the second semester because of poor grades. Another one of my children turned down a scholarship a few semesters into his college career because it was too restrictive. None of my children called home much that first year after leaving home, even though I told them to do so many times. At the time, I wondered if the children even cared how their father and I were faring. As tough as these realities were then, time healed my disappointed heart, and later I became glad these "young adult birds" had learned to fly. I came to realize that my children would learn the consequences of their adult behavior the same way I had learned mine – by experience. It is also the reason they later appreciated the support I had given them when they were younger.

A balanced life, as mentioned in chapter five, is defined in five ways: financially, how we control money; physically, how we can control our health habits; socially, how we interact with friends; emotionally, how we interact with family; and spiritually, how we interact with God. A disciplined Christian balances all five of these elements and is always striving toward improvement in each. We mothers who maintain balance in these areas will lead our children by example, even after they are grown.

The Bible character Joseph loved others and lived a balance life. He handled his duties well on all levels, especially his familial relationships. The verses in Genesis 45 can bring tears to the eyes when Joseph revealed his identity to his brothers. Verse two says, "And he wept aloud: and the Egyptians and the house of Pharaoh heard." Joseph was a good son to his father Jacob. Genesis 46:29 says, "And Joseph made ready his chariot, and went up to meet Israel his father, to Goshen, and presented himself unto him; and he fell on his neck, and wept on his neck a good while."

Think about how Joseph balanced out everything else: he provided well for his two sons, and he sought a blessing for them from his father Jacob. After Jacob died, Joseph lived in Egypt with his sons, his brothers, and his son's children. Genesis 50:23 says "And Joseph saw Ephraim's children of the third generation: the children also of Machir the son Manasseh were brought up upon Joseph's knees." Joseph maintained his faith in God until the end of his life, as evidenced in Genesis 50:25. Joseph made the sons of Israel swear an oath and said, "God will surely visit you, and ye shall carry up my bones from hence." Joseph had a host of friends. Not only did Pharaoh grant him permission to go and bury Jacob in Canaan, but also he allowed the Egyptian officials to accompany Joseph and his brothers.

A mother must also maintain a prayerful attitude about her children's problems.

One of the most famous tightrope walkers who ever lived was Charles Blondin, known to the world during the mid to late 1800s as "The Great Blondin." A Frenchman, he was the first man to cross Niagara Falls on a tightrope, and he wowed audiences throughout Europe, Australia, and the United States. He performed tricks on a tightrope with many props: a wagon, a bicycle, a stove, a table, and a chair; and he implemented the use of each in mid-air. He even carried across on his back his personal assistant, and he once set off a firework show from the middle of the tightrope. Blondin was known for his big heart and his confident personality. He often performed for charity and raised thousands of dollars. He performed hundreds of times and died in his sleep at the age of 73 – a remarkably well-balanced life for a man who centered his entire life on the phenomenon of balance.

When my children were small, they viewed me as incredibly as the world viewed The Great Blondin. This view did not last, though, and only occurred again after they began raising their own children. Now they are complimentary of the sacrifices I have made throughout the years. If most adult children would respect nothing else but the workload that their mothers carried for their sakes, most mothers would feel gratified. If the adult children have a mother who is living out her dreams, is balancing her life, and is happy and charitable, they will be encouraged that there is life after those laborious years of raising children. They will have a first-hand view that life, in Christ, is mostly pleasant despite its hardships and disappointments. Mothers should never underestimate the encouragement her positive example gives to adult children.

My mother-in-law, Louise, is an example of a faithful minister's wife. She sacrificed many things for more than 63 years to fulfill this duty. (At this writing, she and my father-in-law, Bill, are still in the Lord's service.) When Louise turned 77 years old, someone encouraged her to do something for herself and enter a beauty pageant. Her beauty and talent earned her the position of first runner up the first year she entered, and she was crowned Mrs. Calhoun County, Alabama the second year she entered. She turned 80 years old that year, and what fun she had! For the first time in her life, she bought herself evening gowns and indulged in having a great time on her own. She rode on the back of a convertible wearing a full-length mink coat. She traveled around the county and state and sang country and gospel songs in her beautiful alto voice. Her entire family and her friends had fun getting involved with the beauty pageant circuit. "I hope you all can enter a beauty pageant, too," she often tells us. The "encouragement" Louise gave to us showed us how much "courage" is in her character.

Mothers should never underestimate the encouragement her positive example gives to adult children.

╭─────────────────────────────╮
**Scripture Readings
and Prayers**
╰─────────────────────────────╯

1. **Reading**: Proverbs 31:28. The children of the ideal woman in Proverbs 31:28 rose up and called her blessed. This mother is cited for being respectful toward God, financially prudent, charitable, and kind toward her family.

   ❧ **Prayer**: "Dear Heavenly Father, help us search our hearts to see our weaknesses and to strive for balance in our daily living."

2. Mature adulthood, too, is a time to show adult children a good marriage. A quieter, less-stressed home is an opportunity to resolve past issues and to re-bond with each other. When adult children see their parents happy, they have fewer worries about assuming the responsibility to "make" their mother and/or their father happy. Knowing their parents are happy and fulfilled allows adult children to focus on their own marriage, their own children, and their own journey toward fulfillment.

   ❧ **Reading**: Read Malachi 2:13-16. The prophet encourages husbands to "not break faith with the wife of your youth."

🕊 **Prayer:** "Dear Heavenly Father, help us mothers encourage our children to maintain harmonious marriages and homes."

3. In what area of life did each of the following women of the Bible excel?

🕊 **Readings:** Anna (Luke 2:36-38), Tabitha (Acts 9:36-40), and the Shunammite woman (2 Kings 4:8-17).

🕊 **Prayer:** "Dear Heavenly Father, thank You that the gift of mothering extends even beyond our years of raising children."

Mother Oaks
Stand Strong

Minnie Nolan raised ten children of her own and helped raise more than 25 other children, some related and some not.

"It took a lot of hard work and a lot of money to raise that many children. I worked for 30 years in custodial work to have enough money. I had a good attitude, though, toward children. I didn't mind raising them: I just did it. I love children, and even those who weren't mine got to calling me "Mama."

Even Weeping
Willows Smile

When grandson Tyler moved away, Greenbrier Church member Joyce Shaddix had an even harder time than she had had when her three daughters left home decades earlier. "After months of crying about everything related to Tyler," she said, "I decided to start laughing more. I have a choice of crying or laughing, so now I choose laughing."

Notes

Chapter
11

A mother's heart is like the

crystal water in a stream,

sustaining those who partake of it and

gracing the earth with its beauty.

God's love, too, is like all water.

It affects everyone who lives, even those

who are not aware of His love and

even those who reject it.

Those of us who embrace God's love enjoy His many blessings and show our appreciation to Him. There is one great truth between those who acknowledge God in their lives and those who do not: Christians, and especially Christian mothers, know from the Bible that every person is responsible to God for his or her own soul. This truth is a two-edged sword: we are free to choose a godly life, which sets us free to pattern our lives after Jesus, but we cannot choose the path of a godly life for our children who we love almost as much as we love our own souls. This truth brings us joy and breaks our hearts.

The Bible teaches that there are things Christian mothers can do to influence their children for Christ.

In 1 Peter, 3:1,2, the Bible says that husbands "may without the word be won by the conversation of the wives while they behold your chaste conversation." The New International Version translates the Hebrew text as husbands "may be won over without words by the behavior of their wives, when they see the purity and reverence of your lives." The same could apply to a child, family member, or friend.

James 5:16 tells us that "The effectual fervent prayer of a righteous man availeth much." Again, an added meaning is found in the New International Version translation: "The prayer of a righteous man is powerful and effective." Mothers can and should pray for their children's souls.

A Christian mother can even do more: she can realize how her faith has evolved throughout her life and that her children's faith can do likewise. She should practice faith, hope, and love in her attitude concerning her children and allow God to do the rest. She should focus on being a well-rounded Christian woman so God can use her as a tool in His kingdom.

How should a Christian mother cope with the emotional pain that comes from knowing her children have little or no interest in spiritual matters? This is a separate but related problem to influencing her children; yet, this problem is actually easier to solve because the answer lies within a mother's own heart. The metaphor of a stream flowing with God's love is helpful. A Christian mother can imagine the stream filled with the "spiritual stones" of strength, joy, wisdom, trust, and power. The Bible is filled with words that give meaning to these blessings, and these scriptures can lead to emotional healing. A mother who seeks out such scriptures and applies them can heal. A spiritually fulfilled and healed mother can influence her children for Christ better than a bitter, disappointed, and wounded mother.

A spiritually fulfilled and healed mother can influence her children for Christ better than a bitter, disappointed, and wounded mother.

One of the most famous women of the Bible is the Samaritan woman. She went to a well in Samaria and found Jesus there. He used the metaphor of water to show her that through Him she could find God's love. In John 4:10-14, Jesus tells her:

> "If thou knewest the gift of God, and who it is that saith to thee, Give me to drink; thou wouldest have asked of him, and he would have given thee living water. The woman saith unto him, Sir, thou hast nothing to draw with, and the well is deep: from whence then hast thou that living water? Art thou greater than our father Jacob, which gave us the well, and drank thereof himself, and his children, and his cattle? Jesus answered and said unto her, Whosoever drinketh of this water shall thirst again: But whosoever drinketh of the water that I shall give him shall never thirst; but the water that I shall give him shall be in him a well of water springing up into everlasting life."

The spiritual blessings we find in Christ not only produce happiness in this life but also offer us eternal life. The challenge Christians face is that God made us in such a way that we must depend on Him continually to refill us. Sometimes Christian mothers forget this when they face long-term, worrisome, and depressing problems related to their adult children. God has a solution for this problem: He comes first.

In chapter seven of the book that bears his name, the prophet Micah addresses relationship problems between God's people. Sadly, his complaint about the way God's people were treating one another then describes many aspects of modern life. In verses 6 and 7, he says, "For the son dishonoureth the father, the daughter riseth up against her mother, the daughter-in-law against her mother in law; a man's enemies are the men of his own house. Therefore I will look unto the Lord; I will wait for the God of my salvation: my God will hear me."

If we want to be like Jesus and influence others to be like Him, we must make Him our top priority.

During Jesus' ministry, as multitudes followed Him, He began teaching them how much His followers should love Him. In Luke 14:26, He says, "If any man come to me, and hate not his father, and mother, and wife, and children, and brethren, and sisters, yea, and his own life also, he cannot be my disciple." These are strong words from a man who was part of a family and who was meek and kind in personality. Jesus was saying, though, that those who wanted to live the Christian life should weigh the costs. Once we have made the decision to follow Him, we must love Him more than we love ourselves and our own families.

Was Jesus an egotist who wanted everyone to put Him first? Anyone who reads the Bible knows this is not true. Jesus was saying that if we want to be like Jesus and influence others to be like Him, we must make Him our top priority. Otherwise, our initial efforts at following Him will be for nothing. In Luke 14:34,35, Jesus says, "Salt is good: but if the salt have lost his savour, wherewith shall it be seasoned? It is neither fit for the land, nor yet for the dunghill; but men cast it out."

When we love Jesus more than anyone else, our capacity to love others increases.

Here again, these are strong words spoken to people for whom He was willing to die. Jesus loved His hearers. He knew they needed to understand the commitment it would take for them to walk after His ways throughout their lives.

When we fall in love with our newborn children, we mothers make a commitment to live the best we can. We often vow within our hearts to love them throughout their lives. Even more, Jesus wants us to make a commitment to love Him. When we love Jesus more than anyone else, our capacity to love others increases. When we love Jesus supremely, we gain His love, too, to help us raise our children, to love them, and to encourage them to walk with Him. Mothers who give up on God and Jesus when they encounter extreme hardships with their children lose the spiritual source of power and love that can save them and their children.

Let us understand the commitment to allow God's love to flow like living water through our lives and out to those we love.

Scripture Readings and Prayers

1. **Reading:** Revelation 22:1. "And he shewed me a pure river of water of life, clear as crystal, proceeding out of the throne of God and of the Lamb."

    🕊 **Prayer:** "Dear Heavenly Father, allow the water of life to flow from Your heart to ours through Jesus. Empower us with sustaining life available from Your waters, and allow us to demonstrate those waters to our children and to others we love."

2. **Reading:** Revelation 22:17. "And the Spirit and the bride say, Come. And let him that heareth say, Come. And let him that is athirst come. And whosoever will, let him take the water of life freely."

    🕊 **Prayer:** "Dear Heavenly Father, teach us to say 'Come' to You and help us influence our children to say 'Come.' Your spirit enables us to do Your will in many ways."

3. **Reading**: 1 Peter 2:5. The Bible says when we come to Christ, the living stone, "Ye also, as lively stones, are built up a spiritual house, an holy priesthood, to offer up spiritual sacrifices, acceptable to God by Jesus Christ."

♥ **Prayer**: "Dear Heavenly Father, help us mothers to be a part of Your spiritual house and teach those around us to also be a part of the spiritual house. The love we seek to find in You will be visible to others."

Mother Oaks
Stand Strong

As a widow, Judy Patterson suffered from the death of her only son Ken. She remains close to her daughter-in-law and two grandsons.

"Thank you, God, for blessing my life with the gift of Ken, a loving, caring, tender-hearted man who brought so much joy into my life. I can now fill the void daily with wonderful, precious memories he left for me."

Even Weeping
Willows Smile

I keep a box of things belonging to the children and grandchildren when they visit. In the box right now are a swimsuit belonging to six-year-old Tanner, a "choo-choo" train I found at a yard sale for two-year-old Jayden, a stack of books daughter Brianne left behind, a letter that came to the house for son Jeremy, and a pirate hat the children left behind when they played dress up at Maw-Maw's house.

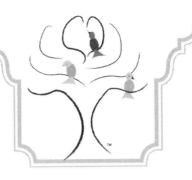

Chapter
12

A mother's heart is like nebulae,

the residual clouds of a star's gases in outer

space that form as it dies.

The memories of the love a mother

shared with her children when

they were small remain behind,

and even though the children are gone

from the home, the love remains.

Look at the night sky. It appears to be still, but actually it is as busy as an intersection. Everything that moves, though, is in slow motion. Stars die, stars are born, objects float in space, comets go by, and everything evolves and revolves.

Some of the most beautiful yet slow movements in the sky are the electrically charged gases that swirl, expand, twist, and circle around a star as it releases energy when dying. We have learned about nebulae thanks to the Hubble telescope. Scientists use colored lenses in the telescope to see the different bands of energy as they are released. The resulting spectacles are among nature's loveliest wonders.

In a similar way, a mother's relationship with her children changes throughout her life. Some aspects of it are dying as others are being born. Perhaps if there were a way to photograph the energy released during these changes, our emotional lives would appear as varied and as charged as nebulae.

One parent in the Bible who knew the extremes of these changes was Job. He was blessed with a wonderful family, but after a strange meeting between God and Satan, Job's family changed. God allowed Job's family to be killed in a terrible storm. Stunned and in disbelief, Job cursed the day of his birth. His heart hurt so deeply that much of the book is taken up with his depression, his fears, his disappointments, his woe, and his hopelessness.

Most of us start out with our own families as Job did. I remember feeling on top of the world with my new family – beautiful children, a loving husband, good health, and prosperity. I often felt like God gave me these blessings because I somehow deserved them. Why else would He bless me so much? Then, over time, things changed. Marital troubles hit. My three teenagers experienced the usual ups and downs of adolescence. I developed fibromyalgia that caused me to ache and feel tired all the time. Career and financial troubles followed, and I felt like Job in Job 29:2 "Oh that I were as in months past, as in the days when God preserved me." I (like most mature adults) woke up one day and wondered why my light-filled life had darkened.

God is great, and we are weak. Sometimes this lesson takes a lifetime to learn. Only then can God's followers be used and blessed by Him in ways they never dreamed.

Job wondered, too, what was left of his life until God reminded him. Chapters 38-41 are accounts of God teaching Job that he was simply a man trying to reason with the Creator of everything. Briefly, in the midst of God's teachings in chapter 40:3-5, Job speaks up. "Behold, I am vile; what shall I answer thee? I will lay mine hand upon my mouth. Once have I spoken; but I will not answer: yea, twice; but I will proceed no further." Job, like all mature followers of God, is humbled. In Job 42:3, he says of his boastful attitude and behavior, "therefore have I uttered that I understood not; things too wonderful for me, which I knew not."

What was Job's answer? He told God in verses 5 and 6, "I have heard of thee by the hearing of the ear: but now mine eye seeth thee. Wherefore I abhor myself, and repent in dust and ashes."

Job came to the same conclusion that all of God's mature followers learn: God is great, and we are weak. Sometimes this lesson takes a lifetime to learn. Only then can God's followers be used and blessed by Him in ways they never dreamed.

In addition to being humbled about who we are and who God is, the Bible in Job 42:10 says Job also "prayed for his friends." Love and awe for God in Job's life went hand in hand with forgiveness toward others. Perhaps this is a good lesson to us that not only should we humble ourselves before God, but also we should forgive those around us who have judged us, who have criticized us, and who have given up on us.

No matter what are a mother's circumstances, good or bad, one thing should remain – a love for God.

When Job learned his lessons, God made him twice as prosperous as before and surrounded him with family and riches. God gave Job an unknown number of sons and three daughters who were more beautiful than any others "in all the land." They enjoyed a rare privilege in those days — an inheritance "among their brethren" (42:15). Even better, Job lived to see his grandchildren to the fourth generation. Job's life was like the slow-moving night sky — an evolving set of circumstances filled with death and life and beauty and, more than anything else, love for God.

No matter what are a mother's circumstances, good or bad, one thing should remain — a love for God. Maybe Job's story tells us that nothing is as important as our love for Him — not our health, not our family, not our financial situation, and not our friends. If we love God, if we humble ourselves to the point of accepting whatever circumstances He asks us to face as mothers, God will draw us to Him and reward us either in this life or in the life to come. It is the state of loving Him, of submitting to Him, of recognizing His greatness, where He wants us to be.

Are our individual circumstances really so important? They may seem that way when everything is perfect. But when bad things happen, what remains? God remains and He helps His children move forward. He helps them serve Him in spite of a broken heart. God heals them, leads them to happiness once again, and brings spiritual joy to their hearts in abundance. Christians can receive even more joy than Job could have known because we now have Jesus: our Saviour who died for us, who took away our sins, and who wants us to live an abundant life. What a blessing we have in Jesus. If we focus on what He did for us and how He wants to bless us spiritually, God may give us more joy than even those born before Jesus' time.

In his first epistle, Peter wrote:

"Blessed be the God and Father of our Lord Jesus Christ, which according to his abundant mercy hath begotten us again unto a lively hope by the resurrection of Jesus Christ from the dead, To an inheritance incorruptible, and undefiled, and that fadeth not away, reserved in heaven for you, Who are kept by the power of God through faith unto salvation ready to be revealed in the last time. Wherein ye greatly rejoice, though now for a season, if need be, ye are in heaviness through manifold temptations: That the trial of your faith, being much more precious than of gold that perisheth, though it be tried with fire, might be found unto praise and honour and glory at the appearing of Jesus Christ: Whom having not seen, ye love; in whom, though now ye see him not, yet believing, ye rejoice with joy unspeakable and full of glory: Receiving the end of your faith, even the salvation of your souls" 1 Peter 1:3-9.

This scripture explains the state of faith for many of my most inspired friends. One couple who visited in my home radiated Christian joy. How surprised I was to learn that they had lost their two adult sons to carbon monoxide poisoning. Another couple I met lost a son to circumstances so mysterious that the police could not explain his death. Their love for God and for each other radiates from them every day. Many of the most loving and joyful people I know, those who seem to live on life's highest mountains, have also experienced life's deepest valleys. They have learned to look beyond their grief and to depend on God's loving and healing nature. They have submitted their own disappointments and pain to God, and they have allowed His love and joy to flood their hearts.

If we go to the source of love, God will change our hearts and make us more like Jesus to influence our adult children and others for Christ.

We mothers can find that same love and joy, no matter what circumstances we face with our children. If we go to the source of love, God will change our hearts and make us more like Jesus to influence our adult children and others for Christ.

Scripture Readings and Prayers

1. **Reading:** 2 Peter 1:19. Jesus living in our hearts is called the Day Star in 2 Peter 1:19, and the subsequent scriptures state that the Holy Spirit moved through men to bring the Word to mankind.

   🕊 **Prayer:** "Dear Heavenly Father, help us as mothers both to look to Jesus as our Day Star and to point others in His direction."

2. **Reading:** Philippians 2:15 says Christians should become blameless and pure children of God and that we should "shine as lights in the world" so that we can carry out the word of life.

   🕊 **Prayer:** "Dear Heavenly Father, help us Christian mothers carry forth Your words of life and love and instill Your truths into the hearts of those around us."

3. **Reading:** In 2 Corinthians 4:6, Paul says that Jesus can shine in our hearts "to give the light of the knowledge of the glory of God." In the previous verse 5, Paul says, "we preach not ourselves, but Christ Jesus the Lord."

   🕊 **Prayer:** "Dear Heavenly Father, help us Christian mothers empty our hearts of pride and ego, and allow Christ's light to shine in our hearts so those we love can see it and be made better by it."

Mother Oaks
Stand Strong

Patricia Ready is a mother who struggled with three miscarriages between the births of her two sons, Spencer, 19, and Will, 13.

"The miscarriages took me by such a surprise after giving birth. I asked, 'why is this happening to me?' and then after the third miscarriage, I couldn't believe it. I then prayed for God's will to be done. After Will was born, a friend gave me a framed poem that is still in his room. It says, 'For this child I have prayed.' My struggle to have a second child gave my life a new meaning."

Even Weeping
Willows Smile

Greenbrier Church member Kim Moss called her son Shane one day after he had been away at college for a while. They discussed several "issues" when she heard Shane pause, sigh heavily, and say, "Mom, I hate to admit this, but you are right most of the time."

Chapter
13

The more I mature in the faith, the more I come to realize that physical blessings are inferior to intangible ones. Physical blessings fade, but the intangible blessings grow stronger each moment for a "striving" Christian. Faith, hope, and love are three of the greatest intangible blessings of all and seem to define the nature of God.

Faith

My childhood faith served me well. From age five, I remember thinking about God often and listening intently in Bible classes where His Word was taught. When I was a youth, I turned to God at a critical period when my heart was deeply wounded over a broken friendship. I remember walking along a cracked sidewalk outside of an annex of my school and sinking toward depression. "Nothing is more real to me at this moment than the sidewalk I am walking on," I thought, "and now it the time to see if God is as real as this sidewalk."

We can become women of faith no matter what the age of our children.

I began praying in earnest and reading the Bible more. I even got a greeting card with a picture of Jesus on it and taped it to the headboard of my bed. My determination to try out my faith put me on the road to a lifelong journey in the realm of God's love. Just after I began the journey, my heart began healing from the broken friendship. God brought into my life soon afterward another friend who later became my husband and has been my partner in faith. Since that time, when I was about 15 years old, God has blessed my life in ways too great to be counted. I have received what I believe to be the reason I was placed on earth — three children. God has gone beyond that blessing, too, and given me grandchildren, a happy marriage, and a life with many friends and extended family. God, through faith, has blessed me more than I deserve.

Biblical Mothers of Faith

An interesting story of faith is found in the first two chapters of Exodus. It is about two Hebrew midwives and Moses' mother. While God's people were in Egypt, Pharaoh grew worried about the large numbers of Hebrews living in his land. He ordered two midwives to kill all boy babies. "The midwives," the Bible says in Exodus 1:17, "feared God and did not as the king of Egypt commanded them, but saved the men children alive." The midwives told Pharaoh that the Hebrew women were so vigorous they delivered babies before the midwives could reach them. Amazingly, Pharaoh believed the lie and did not punish them. God protected them, too, and blessed them because they feared him. Verse 21 says, "[God] made them houses." The NIV Bible translates the meaning as God "gave them families of their own."

Another woman of faith was Moses' mother Jochebed. She was married to a descendent of Levi and gave birth during the time boy babies had been ordered to be killed. She thought of a plan to protect him. She placed her baby in a basket along the Nile River where Pharaoh's daughter would be sure to find it. The mother wisely stationed her daughter Miriam along the Nile, too, to keep an eye on baby Moses, and the mother stayed nearby so when Pharaoh's daughter wanted a wet nurse, Moses' mother got the job. These circumstances are too remarkable to be coincidence. It took a woman of faith to trust God to orchestrate the safety of baby Moses. The story does not stop with Moses living at the palace. Moses' mother taught him, Miriam, and their brother Aaron about God's laws and about how they were God's people. Moses, even though he grew up in the Pharaoh's palace and could have had anything he wanted, aligned himself with his mother's people, the Hebrews. Jochebed taught Moses, Aaron, and Miriam about the ways of God and how to serve Him.

Hope

My favorite scripture is: "Now unto him that is able to do exceeding abundantly above all that we ask or think, according to the power that worketh in us, Unto him be glory in the church by Christ Jesus throughout all ages, world without end" (Ephesians 3:20).

I was once a lonely young Christian because the man who would become my husband went off to college. A Christian neighbor gave me a ride to church, sat with me during worship services, and brought me home each Sunday. As I sat with her, though, I dared to dream of the day my beloved and I would worship together and maybe even have children around us. Since those lonely days of my youth, I have had the privilege of worshipping for many decades with my husband and later with my three children, my grandchildren, my late father, my mother, my mother- and father-in-law, my step-father, my niece and other family members who visit my home from time to time. The concept of Ephesians 3:20 certainly has worked in fulfilling my loneliness and in fulfilling my life in many ways. That scripture has within it the news that "his power that worketh within us" and the news that God will do immeasurably more than we can even hope for. God's hope is alive in my favorite scripture and can override any feeble attempts I make at fulfilling my own dreams.

We can live for God and teach and encourage our children to do the same.

Biblical Mother of Hope

Sarah's lack of hope in Genesis 16 gave rise to Hagar's story of how powerful even a tiny bit of hope might be. Sarah grew weary of waiting on God to give her a child, so she told Hagar to lie with her husband Abram. Hagar gave birth to Ishmael. Both were banished by Sarah after Isaac was born. Imagine the slim hope Hagar had when Abraham sent her and her son into the desert of Beersheba. She and Ishmael drank all of the water and ate all of the food Abraham had given them.

Then Hagar placed her son under a bush and went away because she could not bear to see him die. Chapter 21, verses 17 and 18 say, "And God heard the voice of the lad; and the angel of God called Hagar out of heaven, and said unto her, What aileth thee, Hagar? fear not; for God hath heard the voice of the lad where he is. Arise, lift up the lad, and hold him in thine hand; for I will make him a great nation. And God opened her eyes, and she saw a well of water; and she went, and filled the bottle with water, and gave the lad drink."

Have we ever been so consumed with grief and disappointment that we have not seen God's blessings?

The only thing Hagar hoped for was rescue. What she got was many times greater: her son became the father of many. We mothers must also wonder why God had to open Hagar's eyes so she could see the well of water. Have we ever been so consumed with grief and disappointment that we have not seen God's blessings?

Love

I thought I knew a lot about love after I had my children. Something came along, though, that taught me even more — grandchildren. As each one is born, I marvel at the child's beauty. I cherish even more the brevity of childhood. I focus on getting to know each child's inner and outer beauty, their unique qualities, and each one's special spirit. When I am with my grandchildren, my life feels like a vacation. The grandchildren help me realize how much God loves me and how I need to spend time with Him each day — especially if I can find the time to be still and enjoy His presence.

Motherhood can teach women many things about God, that God can meet her emotional needs and that He loves her more than she loves her children. God loves a mother more than her children and grandchildren love her. God does more for a mother than her children are able to do; that is, God can meet a mother's spiritual needs. He can give her peace, joy, rest in Him, wisdom, forgiveness, the ability to forgive, discipline, love, and all the spiritual blessings of heaven, if she will seek them through His word and through prayer.

Biblical Story of Love

The apostle John knew a woman who was rich in Jesus' love and blessings. He addressed his second letter to her — 2 John. This one-chapter book is addressed to "the elect lady and her children." John was overjoyed to find that Jesus' plan implemented by his apostles had taken effect in this woman's life. He knew the plan was working when he found her children walking in truth, just as the

Father commanded us. John encouraged her in verse 6 to continue walking in obedience to God's commands for "this is love." Let us imagine a woman of Bible times working hard to keep her children neat, clean, well-fed, and concerned for spiritual matters. Let us imagine her and her children interacting with people in that young church in the same manner of love and respect that we see in the lives of our Christian sisters whose children are cherished and are taught God's word. Think of the good that the godly youth in a congregation can do when they are led and taught. This is the type of woman and the type of children to whom John was speaking.

The last verse tells us this woman knew Jesus' love, as did her sister and her sister's children. John was so thrilled to find this rich vein of spiritual love that he wrote to the woman that he wanted to talk with her "face to face, that our joy may be full," verse 12.

As beautiful as letters (and even e-mails) are from family members, nothing is as wonderful as seeing them "face to face." That is how much God loves us and why He has made a way for us to live with Him throughout eternity. Let us all love Him and long to see him face to face. Let us live as verse 9 says and continue "in the doctrine" of Christ so we will have both the Father and the Son. Let us use the faith, hope, and love that God gives us to become who He wants us to be and to encourage others to walk in the light of Jesus.

Mother Oaks Stand Strong

Myra Pugh thought she was facing the hardest challenge of her life when in 2004 she was diagnosed with breast cancer. Then one month later, even before her treatments began, a person who was mentally ill murdered two of her grandchildren and her daughter-in-law. Thanks to God's blessings and the support of her husband, three sons, and five grandchildren, she has overcome the initial period of grief, and she has overcome cancer. She works to assist local law enforcement in their efforts to hire officers trained in the prevention of violence.

Even Weeping Willows Smile

Greenbrier Church member Barbara Hill overheard the conversation between her mother, Evelyn, and her three-year-old grandson, Jackson. He showed the boo-boo on his finger to Evelyn. Barbara saw Evelyn show Jackson a large bruise on her leg in various stages of healing. Barbara worried the sight would scare Jackson. Instead he said, "Wow. Cool colors."

Bibliography

Cooley, Lindell. *The Secret Place of Joy*. Ventura, CA: Regal
    Books from Gospel Light, 2002.

Lindberg, Ann Morrow. *Gifts from the Sea*. New York: Random
    House Large Print in Association with Pantheon
    Books, 1995.

The Holy Bible: King James Version. [Oxford Text Archive.
    New Centre for the Oxford English Dictionary
    (Waterloo). The Humanities Text Initiative,
    University of Michigan's Digital Library Production
    Service, 1994. Sun MicroSystems Inc. grant. 18
    Feb. 1997.] 23 May 2006. <http://www.hti.umich.
    edu/k/kjv>.

The Holy Bible: New International Version. [International Bible
    Society. First print version 1978. Updated 2006.]
    30 May 2006. <http://www.ibs.org>.

"Rear." Def. 5:2 & 6:3. *Webster's New Twentieth Century Dictionary*, 2nd ed. 1966.

The New Analytical Bible and Dictionary of the Bible, John A. Dickson gen. ed. Chicago: John A. Dickson Publishing Co., 1973.

Notes

Notes

Notes

86874

Notes